A FEW GOOD WORDS

A Few Good Words

How Internal Auditors Can Write Better,
More Insightful Reports

Sally F. Cutler

iUniverse, Inc.
New York   Bloomington

A Few Good Words
How Internal Auditors Can Write Better, More Insightful Reports

iUniverse books may be ordered through booksellers or by contacting:

iUniverse
1663 Liberty Drive
Bloomington, IN 47403
www.iuniverse.com
1-800-Authors (1-800-288-4677)

Because of the dynamic nature of the Internet, any Web addresses or links contained in this book may have changed since publication and may no longer be valid.

ISBN: 978-1-4502-0494-1 (sc)
ISBN: 978-1-4502-0493-4 (ebk)

Printed in the United States of America

iUniverse rev. date: 2/23/2010

Also by Sally F. Cutler

Audit Committee Reporting: A Guide for Internal Auditing (The Institute of Internal Auditors Research Foundation, 2009)

Designing and Writing Message-Based Audit Reports (The Institute of Internal Auditors Research Foundation, 2001)

Contents

Part Four: Other Communications

Preface

Yes, internal auditors write. And they write quite a lot. Not only that: the writing they produce delivers critical messages to significant readers—especially today, when issues of risk management, control, and governance have risen to the top of the organizational agenda.

This book is aimed at internal auditors who want to improve their audit reports and their writing overall. It focuses on the strategies and skills needed to explain important and often complex issues and to do so not only clearly and concisely but also tuned to the right pitch.

The book collects columns originally written for *New Perspectives on Risk Management, Control and Governance*, the quarterly journal of The Association of Healthcare Internal Auditors, Inc. Consequently, many of the examples cited refer to healthcare environments and issues. However, any internal auditor will recognize the universal audit-reporting and writing principles presented and will be able to apply them in his or her own environment, be it a corporation, a not-for-profit organization, or a government entity.

Acknowledgements

This book collects a series of columns—also titled *A Few Good Words*—written for *New Perspectives On Healthcare Risk Management, Control And Governance*, the quarterly journal of The Association of Heathcare Internal Auditors, Inc. The columns appeared from 2006 through early 2010.

That organization has been kind enough to grant me permission to publish them in this format. I thank the Association's Board of Directors for allowing me this latitude.

I am grateful in particular to the editor of *New Perspectives*, Ken Spence. He is one of the most encouraging editors I have encountered. He championed the column from the start and has been continuously enthusiastic about it. I'm gratified by his interest in bringing these ideas to the attention of internal auditors. I hope that we two—Ken through his editorial example and I through my advice—have helped a few internal auditors find their way to better, more insightful communications.

Ben Hallam

PART ONE

Audit-Report Content and Organization

Chapter One:
Explaining Significance

You're working on a crucial audit of a high-risk process. You know that the executives and audit committee members who will read your audit report need your assessment of what is significant. They'll ask, "Which findings are most important?" and "What is their relevance to our organization right now?" So, how do you explain the significance of your audit findings, and how do you do so clearly and persuasively?

This chapter describes some key logic skills and a key writing strategy to help you succeed in communicating significance. The logic skills include managing the details of the finding, summarizing the details, and formulating conclusions; the writing strategy is a best practice for organizing these types of information, namely, a top-down approach.

DETAILS, SUMMARIES, CONCLUSIONS

Details

Details are the specifics of the conditions you found. Typically, the details consist of data points: they are specific, factual, and—more often than not—numeric. For example, in an audit of accounts payable, the details of an audit issue related to aging would include the payment-by-payment specifics of the payables tested, such as the identification of each payable, its due date, its payment date, and the number of days aged, if it is past due.

Summaries

Summaries result when you group data by common parameters. In our accounts payable example, you could summarize aged payables by categories of payees, by amounts payable, or by aging, to name three parameters.

When you create such summaries, you use some or all of the following strategies:

- Aggregation: Adding like amounts. For example, you could aggregate the payables amounts aged more than a specified number of days: *Payables aged over 30 days totaled $1.5 million.* Or you could describe the aggregated amount in terms of a percentage: *Payables aged over 30 days represented 60% of the approximately 25,000 payables outstanding.*
- Ranges: Providing the low and high ends of a range. For example, you could provide the span of the aging: *Aged payables ranged from 30 to 150 days past due.*

- Common elements: Combining details that have a parameter in common. For example, you could specify a certain type of payable that was past due: *Of the payables aged over 60 days, 45% were related to third-party service providers.* (Note that this example uses aggregation as well.)

Summaries are necessary in the audit process and in audit reporting. As part of the audit process, summaries help you to see patterns of concern in the data. In audit reporting, summaries help readers to understand the relevance of the data and, in particular, to begin to see and appreciate the risks and their magnitude.

Conclusions

Conclusions are the outgrowth of examining the details and summaries in an organizational context. Conclusions provide audit-report readers with insights based on your auditing expertise and your understanding of internal controls.

To reach conclusions, you need to ask questions about the causes and effects of the patterns in the data. Key questions for reaching such conclusions are, *Why?* and *So what?*

- The *why* question. You ask, *Why did these conditions occur?* Sometimes, the answer to the question is evident from your interviews. Other times, you need to examine the situation further, including asking the audit customer for input on the causes. In our accounts payable aging example, you want to know why payables were aging beyond acceptable parameters. You might conclude that the accounts payable system was insufficient to meet the organization's objectives, that responsibility was not assigned for particular actions related to accounts payable aging, that management was not placing priority (and so not allocating sufficient resources) to meet the organization's expectations for timely payments, or that some other cause was operating.
- The *so what* question. You ask, *What are the consequences of the current conditions and of the ongoing operation of the causes?* To answer these questions, you use your understanding of the risks within the audited entity or process and the risks to the larger organization. In our accounts payable aging example, you might conclude that the organization is losing opportunities for early-payment discounts or is being penalized by late-payment fees and that the organization is risking its reputation with vendors.

THE WRITING STRATEGY

You now are working with three well-defined types of information: details, summaries, and conclusions. However, your logical progression through these types is the inverse of the best strategy for presenting them in the report. That is, your logic started with the details, you then created summaries, and you later formulated conclusions. However, in the audit report, you will use a top-down approach: the conclusions will come first, followed by the appropriate summaries. Details will be included only to emphasize or clarify particularly egregious situations, with the amount of detail based on your organization's culture and your readers' expectations.

Here is an example of how such an audit observation might read for our accounts payable example.

Example

Audit Observation: Accounts Payable Aging

Accounts payable employees have received no formal training in how to resolve aged payables; consequently, the Company has put its reputation with vendors at risk, has paid late-payment penalties, and has missed early-discount opportunities.

Using data analysis, we found that 25% of the approximately 35,400 outstanding payables were aged more than 45 days, which is the maximum aging stipulated by the Company's accounts payable procedures. The aging ranged from 46 to 198 days, and these aged payables totaled $22.3 million.

For 75% of the aged payables, no resolution efforts had been made for at least 7 days, and for the most aged payable, no resolution efforts had been made for 32 days.

Between January 1 and June 30, 20xx, the Company paid approximately $145,000 in late-payment fees. In addition, we estimate that the Company lost the opportunity to take early-payment discounts of approximately $135,000, had the Company chosen to do so.

Recommendation 1: Train the accounts payable staff in how to resolve aged payables.

Recommendation 2: Target the most significantly aged payables for the earliest resolution.

This writing strategy—leading with the conclusions—is a best practice for two reasons. One is related to emphasis, and the other is related to comprehension. Placing the conclusions first emphasizes them because readers perceive that what comes first is more important than what follows. Placing the conclusions first also enhances comprehension because readers understand summaries and the details better when the big-picture conclusions come first.

You may have experienced this comprehension effect in your own reading, encountering both positive and negative examples. In fact, many documents attend to the comprehension issue by providing elements such as executive summaries, abstracts, and chapter summaries (in textbooks). Even a table of contents enhances comprehension (although it rarely delivers conclusions).

You can train yourself to write in this top-down style even if it does not come naturally. One way to do so is to recognize the logical distinctions among details, summaries, and conclusions and then to conscientiously write them as separate statements. Once you have these statements drafted, you can move them into the correct positions, adding transitions to tie the ideas together. For example, notice the transitions in our accounts payable aging observation: *consequently, and, in addition*. (The semicolon in the first sentence of the observation also serves as a kind of transition.)

You've applied the logical skills related to details, summaries, and conclusions, and you've employ the top-down writing strategy. The resulting report clearly and persuasively makes the case for action—the ultimate test of your ability to explain significance.

Chapter Two:
Using Organizing Tools

You've just completed a complex audit. It covers a number of scope areas, and you have a good deal of important information to present—so much, in fact, that you're feeling overwhelmed about how to put it all together. Your standard report format helps you organize the document overall, but within each section, you're struggling to get the information into a clear, logical sequence. So what tools might you use to help you sort out your information?

This chapter describes pre-writing tools you can use to organize ideas and information before you start drafting, thus saving writing time and revision effort. Included is that old standard the outline as well as a free-form tool called a mind map; also included is the notion that information can be shaped into various logical patterns.

OUTLINES

Many of us were taught to use an outline as a pre-writing tool. For example, you may have been required to submit an outline along with or in advance of a school writing assignment.

An outline is an ideal way to display two organizational characteristics: hierarchy and sequence.

Hierarchy

The outline's premise is that information and ideas can be broken into major topics, the major topics can be broken into sub-topics, and so on. Doing so creates hierarchy within the information. An outline uses indentation and numbering to display this hierarchy. Thus, one outlining advantage is the requirement that you establish hierarchy within your information, finding the relationship of smaller issues to larger ones and finding a place for the details.

Sequence

An outline also relies on the organizing principle of sequence: listing information in the order in which you intend to present it in the full write-up. Sequence shows the flow of the information. Thus, the second outlining advantage is the requirement that you establish the sequence of your information— the logical way you will lead the reader through.

Types of outlines

Two outline variations are the standard outline and the sentence outline, each with its own advantages.

The entries in a standard outline are phrases, used as shorthand representations of information. A standard outline works well for a solo writer, who is familiar with what each phrase represents and who uses the outline as a quick way to develop hierarchy and sequence. Here is an example of a standard outline.

Example

Audit Finding: Sales Commissions
1. Lack of education and of monitoring = inconsistent commission standards
    1.1. Regional variations
    1.2. Individual variations
2. Inconsistently paid commissions
    2.1. Western region underpayment error: $975,000
    2.2. Risks to the organization
        2.2.1. Inequitable treatment of sales personnel
        2.2.2. Possibility of fraud (not found)
    2.3. Specifics
        2.3.1. Sales person A: underpayment of $550,000
        2.3.2. Sales person B: underpayment of $257,000
        2.3.3. Sales person C: underpayment of $168,000
3. Recommendations
    3.1. Train management on commission standards
    3.2. Monitor closely
    3.3. Pay sales personnel amounts owed

The entries in a sentence outline are full sentences. A sentence outline works well for collaborating writers, who need the clarity that full sentences provide. A sentence outline also is useful for a writer seeking a reviewer's or editor's input before drafting. Finally, a sentence outline is useful as a stepping stone for a solo writer experiencing a writing block: the sentence outline closes in on the draft but feels less intimidating. Here is an example of a sentence outline based on the standard outline shown above.

Example

Audit Finding: Sales Commissions
1. Lack of management education and of management monitoring has led to inconsistent commission standards being used.
   1.1 The western region has not followed sales commission standards.
   1.2 Sales by individuals within the western region have been treated differently.
2. Commissions have not been paid consistently.
   2.1 We calculated an underpayment error within the Western Region is $975,000.
   2.2 The organization is exposed to two risks:
      2.2.1 Inequitable treatment of sales personnel could result in employee dissatisfaction and loss of experienced sales people.
      2.2.2 Although we found no fraud, fraud could have been committed and would have been difficult to detect.
   2.3 Underpayments totaled as follows:
      2.3.1 Sales person A was underpaid $550,000.
      2.3.2 Sales person B was underpaid $257,000.
      2.3.3 Sales person C was underpaid $168,000.
3. We are making three recommendations:
   3.1 Train all management on commission standards.
   3.2 Monitor western region commissions closely.
   3.3 Pay sales personnel the amounts owed them.

The challenge of outlines

In theory, if you've fully considered the material at hand, an outline is an ideal pre-writing tool for developing hierarchy and sequence. In practice, however, you may find it difficult to envision hierarchy and sequence simultaneously. Your outline may look sound, but the writing may prove the hierarchy to be faulty or the sequence to be illogical. For these reasons, you may find an outline to be a cumbersome pre-writing tool.

MIND MAPS

A mind map has one organizing purpose: to develop hierarchy.

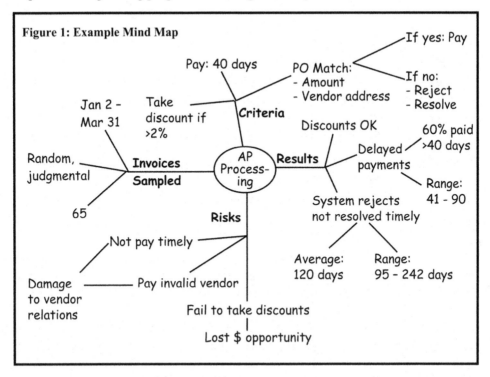

Figure 1: Example Mind Map

When you make a mind map, you do not develop sequence.

To make a mind map, you begin with your main topic or main message in the center circle. Then, you add branches, sub-branches, sub-sub-branches, and so forth. You may skip around the mind map, and you need not worry about the ultimate sequence of the information. Your aim is to create clusters of information, with the branching and sub-branching showing the hierarchy.

You may find a mind map useful as a stand-alone pre-writing tool. You may also find you can first make a mind map and then make an outline based on the mind map, using the mind map to develop the hierarchy and the outline to develop the sequence.

PATTERNS

Outlines and mind maps enable you to envision the logic within your information, and you will find that various types of logic will be present. Specifically, these five patterns are common within internal audit reports: chronology, priority, comparison, cause-and-effect, and location.

Chronology pattern

Chronology (or chronological order) is the logic of time: What happened first, next, and finally? Using chronology, you place information in time order, generally from first to last.

In an internal audit report, chronology is useful for describing processes as well as events. Here are examples of chronology used for the steps in a process and for a description of how a fraud could be committed.

Examples

The ER technician gathers the information from the patient or other responsible party and enters the information into the system. The system automatically assigns an event number and checks for missing or conflicting data. The system flags the record as an open event and assigns a priority code based on the data entered.

Buyers had access to the vendor system and could set up a fictitious vendor in the system. A buyer then could create a purchase order, create a goods-received notice, and authorize payment to the fictitious vendor.

Priority pattern

Priority is the logic of importance: Among these non-time-dependent issues, which is most important, and how do the rest follow in decreasing order of importance? Using priority, you place information in order based on significance.

In an internal audit report, priority is useful for sequencing the audit observations within the report and for sequencing issues within each observation. Here is an example of an audit observation that uses priority.

Example

The contracting process was deficient in three ways. Most importantly, the legal department was not required to review contracts containing non-standard clauses; we found that none of these contracts had been reviewed by legal. Also, contractors were able to begin work before contracts were executed; we found five contractors performed work billed at a total of $4.3 million without signed contracts. Finally, contracts did not contain right-to-audit clauses; we found that no contracts contained such clauses.

Notice that a priority pattern is flexible: you can re-order the issues if your decision about priority changes.

Comparison pattern

Comparison is the logic of differences: How do two or more things differ? Using comparison, you highlight such differences.

In an internal audit report, comparison is useful for describing how conditions differ from criteria. Here is an example of a comparison between criteria and conditions found.

Example

Personnel policy requires that all employees receive initial diversity training within three months of hiring, with annual updates thereafter. In 20xx, however, 54 of the new hires (23%) did not receive such training within three months of their hiring date, and 5 of these never received initial training. Furthermore, 75% of current employees have failed to attend at least one annual update session.

Cause-and-effect pattern

Cause-and-effect is the logic of causality: Why did something occur, and what were the consequences? Using cause-and-effect, you make a causal connection between one event or series of events and another, be it actual or potential.

In an internal audit report, cause-and-effect is useful for raising higher-level issues, helping readers to understand root causes and risks. Thus, cause-and-effect is particularly useful in executive summaries. Here is an example of a high-level conclusion that uses a cause-and-effect pattern.

Example

The lack of a systematic, disciplined approach to disaster-recovery planning has put at risk the organization's ability to meet contractual customer requirements.

Location pattern

Location is the logic of place: Where are things situated, or where did events occur? Using location, you present similar information for each location described, sometimes ordering the locations geographically and sometimes by some form of priority (for example, largest to smallest or oldest to newest).

In an internal audit report, location is useful when the audit covers more than one location and when the readers need to see results distinguished by location. Here is an example using a location pattern to describe related facilities.

Example

All three urgent-care facilities exceeded the target patient-waiting time of 20 minutes. The average waiting time at the East facility was 45 minutes; at the West facility, 37 minutes; and at the Downtown facility, 32 minutes.

The power of patterns

Before drafting, you can consider which patterns—that is, which types of logic—best suit your information and your message. Your report may have one overall pattern and then several sub-patterns.

These patterns should be evident within each report section and within each paragraph. Considering the patterns in advance, you can ensure that the writing emphasizes the logic, enabling your reader readily to grasp the information. Furthermore, you can streamline your own writing process by using patterns as an organizing tool.

DIFFERENT TOOLS FOR DIFFERENT WRITERS

Outlines, mind maps, and patterns—you may find that your own thinking style makes one of these tools most appealing. For some, the structure of an outline is reassuring; for others, the free-form qualities of the mind map resonate; and for still others, the ability to formulate a logical pattern enables smooth drafting. You may find it worthwhile to experiment—to try out these tools in different writing situations—to see which of them appeals most to you and gives you the greatest pre-writing advantage.

By using organizing tools, you've worked through and managed all that good information you found during the audit engagement, easing the writing task and leading to a higher-quality, easier-to-follow report.

Chapter Three:
Solving the Goldilocks Dilemma

You've done a lot of work on your most recent audit, and you have a good amount of complex information to convey. Your audit customer wants to know what you found, and you need to support your conclusions. Still, you know that many of your report's readers—and especially those at the executive and audit committee levels—don't want or need to see a lot of details. So, you're struggling to decide how much detail to include.

This chapter suggests ways to deal with what we might call the Goldilocks dilemma: not too much, not too little, but just right.

THE CHALLENGE

You may recall that, in the Goldilocks story, the title character has entered the three bears' house and is trying out their chairs, bowls of porridge, and beds to see which ones are right for her. Some of the chairs and beds are too big, some are too small, but some are *just right*.

As a writer, you too are seeking the *just right* amount of information and level of detail to include in your reports. If you include too much, you lose the readers and bury your messages; if you include too little, you raise more questions than you answer.

As with all other writing decisions, the decision about the level of detail should be based on the readers' needs. That is, if you are aiming to have the readers agree with your conclusions, the level of detail should provide sound, logical support from the readers' perspective.

LEVELS OF DETAIL

One starting point for addressing this challenge is to see information at three levels of detail: granular, mid-level, and high-level.

- Granular detail is raw data. Consider the example of a spreadsheet that captures accounts payable information for every invoice you paid to every vendor in the past six months. The spreadsheet might contain each vendor's name, vendor number, and address; each invoice number, its corresponding purchase-order number, the amount paid, and the payment date; and the people authorizing payments.
- Mid-level information shows groupings within the raw data. For our spreadsheet example, the mid-level information might include the grand total paid to all vendors during the period, the total

paid to each vendor, the number of invoices (if any) for which the purchase-order field is empty, and other such aggregated information.

- High-level information calls out a meaningful pattern from the raw data. In our accounts payable spreadsheet, we might find that all the invoices with empty purchase-order fields are for one vendor and that the amounts for these invoices are all exactly $50,000—even though all other invoices paid to this vendor are under $20,000 and none are for round-number amounts.

TOO MUCH DETAIL

Confronted with the Goldilocks dilemma, many writers default to the granular level. They may do this for several reasons.

First, many writers have the misconception that granular detail is essential for less-technical readers. That is, the writer mistakenly assumes that such readers need more explanation in order to understand a complex issue. In fact, the opposite is true: the more complex the issue, the less detail these less-technical readers want and need. They find granular detail confusing, not illuminating.

Second, some writers think that granular detail will impress the reader with the thoroughness of the audit. Unfortunately, granular detail often has a different effect: readers justifiably feel that the writer has abdicated his or her responsibility, making the reader do all the work of sorting through and making sense out of the details.

TOO LITTLE DETAIL

Providing too little detail results in gaps in the logic and questions from your readers. Thus, the readers cannot reach the conclusions you reached.

In considering what is logically necessary, we need to start with definitions and examples of two types of conclusions:

- Inductive conclusions are reached through the assembly of supporting details or evidence. Say you have evidence that a creature has white feathers and a yellow bill, waddles when it walks, lays eggs, and makes a quacking sound. Most people will conclude that this is a duck (and a female one, at that). We say that the conclusion is induced from the details.
- Deductive conclusions are reached by applying general principles. Say you have a general principle that all ducks can swim, and you know that the creature you have is a duck. Most people will reach the deductive conclusion that the creature you have can swim. We say that the conclusion is deduced by applying the general principle to the evidence.

You reach inductive and deductive conclusions throughout your audits. For example, you reach an inductive conclusion when you examine data showing multiple instances of invoices being paid without purchase orders and conclude that the payment process does not have sufficient controls to prevent such activity. You reach a deductive conclusion when you apply the principle of separation of duties to the evidence of a condition where one person has the ability to both issue purchase orders and approve payments.

How does understanding the logic of conclusions help you resolve the Goldilocks dilemma? It helps by enabling you to anticipate when people may disagree with your conclusions. Specifically, for an inductive conclusion, people may disagree about the sufficiency of the evidence. Some people will accept nothing less than DNA evidence before agreeing with your conclusion that your white-feathered, yellow-billed, waddling, egg-laying, quacking creature is a duck. For a deductive conclusion, people may disagree about the validity or applicability of the principle. Some people may not believe that all ducks can swim, so they will not find your conclusion valid that your duck must be able to swim.

Consider how such disagreements might appear during an audit. Your conclusion that controls are lacking in an accounts payable process might be challenged if you had evidence of only one invoice paid without a purchase order. That is, you would be challenged on the sufficiency of your evidence. Your conclusion about the need to separate duties might be challenged if your audit customer or others had little understanding of the principle of separation of duties, or if they believed the principle did not apply to their process.

By understanding how disagreements arise, you can adjust the level of detail in your reports. Consider asking yourself these questions:

- For a deductive conclusion: Have I provided the readers with sufficient evidence? Are granular details necessary to support the conclusion? Is mid-level information helpful? If so, which granular details or what mid-level information?
- For an inductive conclusion: Will my readers accept the validity and applicability of the general principle or principles I used to reach my conclusion? To be persuasive, do I need to provide granular detail about the validity of the principle and its applicability to the audit issue? Would mid-level information about the principle be helpful? If so, which granular details or what mid-level information?

JUST RIGHT LEVELS OF DETAIL

For most reports, different readers need different levels of information. Thus, you should combine levels to meet their disparate needs. Here is how the detail may be managed in various report sections:

- Executive summary: high-level information
- Audit observations: high-level and mid-level information, which may introduce selected granular details
- Appendices (if used): granular details

In the executive summary, focusing on high-level information allows you to convey the essential messages. Of course, sometimes a single granular detail may be truly significant or may perfectly illustrate a message. If so, consider including that granular detail in the executive summary.

In the audit observations, layering of information is effective. In particular, you can use high-level or mid-level information to introduce selected granular information. This approach has two advantages. First, it enables better understanding of the granular details: the high-level or mid-level introduction provides a framework for the details. Second, this approach enables readers to skim the report and still take away an understanding of the issues. Here is an example of high-level information layered with mid-level information and then granular detail.

Example

Purchase orders existed for all invoices except those of one vendor, a provider of consulting services. Specifically, between January 1, 20xx and March 31, 20xx, Vendor X was paid a total of $1.25 million on 35 invoices, 20 of which had no corresponding purchase orders. Furthermore, these 20 invoices all were for an even $50,000, while none of the 15 invoices supported by purchase orders was for more than $18,000. One of the unsupported invoices (February 1, 20xx) included no description of the services provided.

In appendices (if they are used), providing the granular detail offers the full picture for technical readers and those with a keen interest in the issues. Granular detail in appendices is particularly effective when presented using well-constructed graphs, charts, and tables.

Goldilocks may have struggled to find what was "just right," but you've been able to make good decisions about the level of detail by asking that essential question, "What do the readers need to know?" Then, you've used appropriate levels of granular, mid-level, and high-level information. You've confident that the resulting report will robustly support your conclusions without burying the messages with too much detail.

Chapter Four:
Writing Report Opinions

Until now, you've issued your reports without a formal "opinion." You've taken this approach because you believe it enables you to more effectively persuade management to take action. But now your audit committee wants you to include a formal opinion—and an overall rating—on every report. You're wondering how you can meet the audit committee's need without alienating your audit customers, with whom you have steadily been building a trusting and productive relationship.

This chapter defines whole-report opinions and explores why and how internal auditors write them. Included are the pros and cons of rating systems: their value for audit committees and executives as well as their potential to create conflicts with management. Finally, the chapter addresses multi-report opinions—an increasingly frequent audit-committee request. The chapter places these ideas in the context of recent guidance on opinion writing.

WHOLE-REPORT (MICRO) *OPINIONS*

Whole-report opinions are high-level conclusions about the overall import of the observations within a single report. They may be called *micro* opinions to distinguish them from opinions that span multiple reports, which may be called *macro* opinions.

The guidance provided by The Institute of Internal Auditors says that whole-report opinions are *evaluations of the effects of observations and recommendations* and that they *put the observations and recommendations in perspective based on their overall implications* (The Institute of Internal Auditors, *International Professional Practices Framework*, Practice Advisory associated with IPPF 2410.A1). This language points to a crucial aspect of a whole-report opinion, namely, that it is more than a summary. Consider this situation:

You audited procurement, and one aspect you looked at was background checks on contract personnel, including those providing patient services. You have a spreadsheet with data for a sample of 25 such active contract personnel. The spreadsheet documents whether a background check was conducted for each contractor and whether all components of the background check were completed. The spreadsheet shows that background checks were not conducted for Contractors A and B; it also shows that drug testing—a required aspect of the background check—was pending for Contractors C, D, and E. All five of these contractors were providing services.

One possible summary of this detail is, *We sampled 25 active contract personnel providing patient services and found 5 for whom required background checks either were not conducted or were incomplete.*

However, a conclusion about the findings goes further than this summary. For example, a conclusion might say, *Patients may have been put at risk because background checks on some contract personnel providing patient services either were not performed or were incomplete.* Moreover, if supported by interviews and observations, your conclusion might go on to say something like, *Deficiencies in performing background checks resulted from a lack of centrally assigned responsibility for this activity, with departments interpreting the requirements in differing ways.*

Conclusions, then, are broader statements—founded on facts—that rise to the level of describing the effects (risks) and causes of the conditions you found.

A whole-report conclusion—an opinion—describes the themes or commonalities across an entire report. Thus, an opinion focuses on higher-level and often systemic issues revealed by the audit. An opinion reaches to the level of providing a consolidated view of the *overall implications* of the observations.

For example, say that your audit of procurement found not only differing interpretations related to background checks but also conflicting interpretations of other procurement requirements. Your overall conclusion could be that the organization risked patient safety and operating effectiveness by using inappropriate vendors in essential and non-essential areas because procurement management was not coordinating procurement activities (a control-environment issue) and was not communicating effectively with management in other areas of the organization.

RATING SYSTEM PROS AND CONS

Positive impacts of ratings

When used, a whole-report rating system is part of the auditor's opinion. It consolidates the opinion into an easy-to-grasp phrase, numeric value, or color. Thus, audit committees and executive readers favor rating systems, and the reasons are easy to see:

- A rating system provides an instant view of the auditor's opinion.
- The rating provides context for everything else in the report, both in terms of significance and urgency.
- Reports can be more easily compared, as can audit results for units across the organization.
- Ratings help management set priorities.

Common and not-so-common rating systems

Most such systems use three ratings. They may be given descriptors, most often *unsatisfactory*, *needs improvement*, and *satisfactory*. Alternatively, they may be numbered or assigned colors. (The traffic-light colors of *red, yellow,* and *green* are common.) This three-point system is straightforward and communicates a simple range within the opinion.

Organizations aiming for more clarity in the middle category of a three-point system may split the *needs improvement* rating. The new descriptors may be *needs significant improvement* and *needs improvement*, or they may be *mostly unsatisfactory* and *mostly satisfactory*. A color-based system may add *orange* between *yellow* and *red*.

Some innovative organizations have enhanced their report ratings by displaying other dimensions along with the report rating. They do so to provide the audit committee and senior executives with a comprehensive view of the control environment. One such organization provides these three dimensions:

- Inherent risk (*high, medium, low*). This is the risk that placed the audit on the audit plan in the first place.
- Residual risk, which is the actual report rating (*unsatisfactory, needs improvement, satisfactory*). This rating is based on the issues found during the audit.
- Management awareness (*high, medium, low*). This rating is based on management's self-identification of issues—and resulting actions—before the audit began as well as on whether issues in the report are repeat issues.

Whatever the rating system, you'll be wise to periodically check that the ratings continue to function in communicating relative concern. Thus, unless an organization is exceptional, we would expect a distribution of ratings—albeit neither an even distribution nor a bell-shaped curve. A rating system needs revision if, for example, all or almost all reports receive a *needs improvement* rating, with *unsatisfactory* or *satisfactory* ratings never or rarely used.

Formulation of the rating

A whole-report rating is arrived at by tempering objective criteria with professional judgment. Objective criteria may include any or all of the following:

- The number of high-priority observations in the report
- The nature and extent of the risks (for example, pervasive health-and-safety issues weighing more heavily than sporadic accounting errors)
- The nature and extent of the causes (for example, findings resulting from intentional bypasses weighing more heavily than those resulting from staff making one-off errors)
- Whether issues found are repeat issues from previous audits

Once ratings criteria are established, however, auditors must add perspective and be willing to use judgment in making the final rating decision. Important factors include the auditor's perception of management responsiveness and any compounding of risks across observations.

Negative impacts of ratings

Audit committees and executives favor ratings, but management often does not. The very clarity that makes ratings attractive to audit committees and executives makes ratings unattractive to management audit customers. They may feel that ratings oversimplify complex issues, are unfairly judgmental, or suppress audit-customer efforts to rectify problems.

The tensions over ratings can impact the auditor's relationship with the audit customer. We auditors claim to be helping management achieve better governance, risk management, and controls, but then we apply a rating—a grade—to management's efforts. The rating may feel like punishment to management.

Furthermore, some auditors find that management is fixated on improving the report rating, taking the focus off the issues themselves. In some organizations, the negotiation of the rating obstructs report issuance; in others, where ratings have consequences for job security and careers, escalations and delays can be common.

Finally, many auditors must interact with audit customers on repeated engagements, and relationships can be poisoned by protracted ratings battles. Auditors focused on adding value through management action may question how ratings move the organization in a productive direction.

To rate or not to rate

In deciding whether or not to rate your reports, you should weigh a number of factors:

Your organization

- What is your organization's culture? Other areas of your organization may commonly rate activities and outcomes; if so, internal audit will better align with the organization by adopting ratings.
- How large is your organization? The more lines of business, operating units, and geographies within your organization, the more useful ratings are.
- How much change is your organization undergoing? The more your organization is changing, the more useful ratings are.

Your audit committee

- Does your audit committee see all of the audit reports, some of them, or multi-report summaries only? Ratings are particularly useful in developing multi-report summaries.
- How engaged is your audit committee? Ratings can grab the attention of a disengaged audit committee.

Your internal audit function

- How many audits do you conduct? The more audits you conduct, the more useful ratings are.
- How responsive is management in closing issues? Ratings are useful in helping management see the priority of closure.

MULTI-REPORT (MACRO) *OPINIONS*

The convergence of financial and operational pressures on organizations has increased interest in internal audit offering multi-report (macro) *Opinions*. Internal audit functions have long summarized results for their audit committees; recently, however, audit committees have sought an overall opinion from internal audit (as they do from external financial auditors). Internal audit is being asked to express an overall (macro) opinion on governance, risk management, internal controls, the control environment, compliance, and so forth.

Your decision to provide such an opinion should be based on considerations of intent, audit coverage, and clarity. In 2009, The Institute of Internal Auditors provided an in-depth discussion of such considerations. (See The Institute of Internal Auditor's *Practice Guide: Formulating and Expressing Opinions.*) In brief, these considerations include the following:

- The purpose of the macro opinion
- Whether the audit period and testing timelines support a macro opinion
- Whether the audit work and audit evidence are sufficient to support a macro opinion
- The criteria on which the macro opinion is based
- The organization's risk appetite related to the criteria
- Clear definitions of the terms used to express the macro opinion

After discussions with the audit committee and executive management, you've reached a consensus on whole-report opinions, including a rating system. All stakeholders—audit committee, executive management, and management—are clear about how internal audit will develop the opinion and the rating and how these components will be used by management and the audit committee. You are committed to using this approach to deliver crisper messages to all of these stakeholders. And although your audit committee is not yet asking for a "macro" opinion, you are confident that, if and when they do, you will be able to develop a firm foundation for communicating at that level as well.

PART TWO

Audit-Report Quality

Chapter One:
Making Writing Concise

A writer looks over the comments you've added to her document. They suggest that she make the writing more concise by removing information, deleting words, and shortening sentences. "But I'll insult my readers," she says, "They'll think I'm talking down to them. They need to understand all this, and they ought to be able to read what I've written because they're all college graduates." This writer has confused conciseness with over-simplification. She has also made a classic error: she has tasked the reader with the responsibility for understanding rather than owning that responsibility herself.

This chapter offers four strategies for conciseness:

- Focus on what the readers want and need.
- Include only necessary information.
- Use words economically.
- Control sentence length.

A FOCUS ON WHAT THE READERS WANT AND NEED

To distinguish wanted from unwanted and needed from unneeded information, you need first to understand your readers. Specifically, you should identify how they will use the document, determine their levels of understanding, and assess their possible reactions.

Sometimes you can readily predict how readers will use a document; other times, the task is harder. For example, readers of an email announcing a meeting will use the email to put the meeting on their calendars and to prepare the meeting. Thus, they want and need to know where and when the meeting will take place, what topics it will cover, and what is expected of them. When the prediction about document use is harder, you need to imagine yourself into the readers' place—a good trick for any writer to learn. You may also need to ask for insights from others who better understand the readers and their roles.

The readers' levels of understanding help us to know how much or how little detail they need. Readers with a high level of technical understand usually want and need more detail; those with a lower level of understanding usually want and need less. This equation—high level equals more detail, and low level equals less detail—is poorly understood by many writers. In fact, some writers think they need to explain more to readers with lower levels of understanding, and they load documents with technical information beyond the reader's reach and outside the reader's attention span. The key is to provide those details that illuminate the messages, not to attempt to bring the non-technical reader to the same level of technical understanding possessed by the writer. (See *Part One, Chapter Three: Solving the Goldilocks Dilemma* for more on handling levels of detail.)

The readers' anticipated reactions to the document also influence what they want and need. Receptive readers usually need less persuasion, and including too many details may make us appear unsure of ourselves. Skeptical readers need even-handed presentations and explanations. Hostile readers may need more explanation and soothing words.

NECESSARY INFORMATION

As you draft a document, you may state the obvious, impeding conciseness. For example, a report heading *Recommendations* need not be followed by the sentence, *We recommend the following actions.*

Consider this longer example of unnecessary information.

> *Example*
>
> The internal audit department has adopted a risk-based approach to each audit. A risk-based approach to internal auditing is a best practice in the field of internal auditing. Using a risk-based approach, we first work with the audit client to identify the overall risks within the process. Next, we develop a rating based on the likelihood of the risk occurring and the potential impact of a risk *event*. We then focus the internal audit on the highest risk areas as identified by the department's risk-based approach to internal auditing.

Repetition of key terms (in the example, the word *risk*) is an effective strategy for coherence, but the repeated definitions in this example are unnecessary. Here is a revision that reduces the paragraph from 89 to 71 words.

> *Example*
>
> The internal audit department has adopted a risk-based approach to each audit. This approach is a best practice in the field of internal auditing. We first work with the audit client to identify the overall risks within the process. Next, we develop a rating based on the likelihood of the risk occurring and the potential impact of a risk *event*. We then focus the internal audit on the highest risk areas.

WORD ECONOMY

English is wonderfully flexible, with various ways of expressing a single idea. Unfortunately, such flexibility can lead to sentences loaded up with unnecessary words and phrases. Here are four common problems that impede word economy:

- Habitual expressions that add no value
- Redundancies
- *There is...* constructions
- Noun constructions where verbs will do

Habitual expressions take up space without adding content, and English is full of them. Consider the following revisions for habitual expressions.

> *Examples*
>
> Original: In order to prevent errors in order processing, four specific changes will be made in the procedures.
>
> Revision: To prevent errors in order processing, four changes will be made in the procedures.
>
> Original: The department is in the process of revising the personnel manual.
>
> Revision: The department is revising the personnel manual.

Redundancies occur when two words or phrases say the same thing or when one idea is implicit in another. Consider the following revisions for redundancies.

> *Examples*
>
> Original: The manager returned the report back to the auditor for changes.
>
> Revision: The manager returned the report to the auditor for changes.
>
> Original: The changes will build on the self-assessment foundation that is already in place.
>
> Revision: The changes will build on the self-assessment foundation.
>
> Original: Three separate electrical poles are located in close proximity to the emergency exit.
>
> Revision: Three electrical poles are located close to the emergency exit.

Constructions that begin *There is...* (or any variation in number or tense) almost always benefit from revision. Consider the following revisions for *There is...* constructions.

Examples

Original: There were errors in the credit verification reports.

Revision: The credit verification reports contained errors.

Original: There were two reasons given for the lack of documentation.

Revision: Two reasons were given for the lack of documentation.

Original: There are instances in which the lack of duplicate-payment controls resulted in vendor overpayments.

Revision: The lack of duplicate-payment controls resulted in vendor overpayments.

Using noun constructions where verbs will do results in longer, less vivid expressions. Consider the following revisions to changes noun constructions to verb constructions.

Examples

Original: In 20xx, the Board gave consideration to merging the two divisions.

Revision: In 20xx, the Board considered merging the two divisions.

Original: The consultant made a recommendation for ways to begin the documentation of the Sarbanes-Oxley project.

Revision: The consultant recommended ways to begin documenting the Sarbanes-Oxley project.

Original: We recommend the department undertake revisions in the task descriptions used to provide training to new employees.

Revision: We recommend the department revise the task descriptions used to train new employees.

SENTENCE LENGTH

Long sentences give the impression that the writing lacks conciseness—even when the writer has used all of the strategies discussed so far. The information may be necessary, and the words may be used economically. However, writing dominated by long sentences fatigues the readers and taxes their attention.

Sentences that average 15 to 20 words will be read easily by most readers. Hitting this average does not ensure success: as we have seen, even short sentences can lack conciseness. However, routinely exceeding this length makes reading difficult. (See *Part Two, Chapter Two: Using Sentence Metrics to Improve Clarity* for more on sentence length.)

That struggling writer now knows that conciseness is built from the top down: understanding what readers want and need. She also knows to include only necessary information, to use words economically, and to break up long sentences. She's confident that, with practice, she can use these strategies. The result will be a crisp, vivid document that is easy to read—even when it deals with complex, technical issues.

Chapter Two:
Using Sentence Measurements to Improve Clarity

On the screen in front of you is the fourth draft of your latest report. Despite your efforts, you have the troubling sense that the writing is not as crisp and clear as it could be. In fact, every time you read the report, you change something. You wonder if there isn't some objective way to assess the clarity of your own writing.

This chapter explores four objective measurements of sentence clarity: sentence length, subject-to-verb distance, length of introductory elements, and number of prepositional phrases in a row. These measurements have the potential to enhance your writing demonstrably, to smooth out the reading, and to enable you to present information and ideas more clearly.

CAN YOU REALLY MEASURE CLARITY?

The answer is *yes…and no*. Measurements alone cannot guarantee clear writing. Effective message placement, logical organization, and coherence—these are the foundations of clear writing. Absent these characteristics, revisions based on objective measurements will only superficially clear up the writing.

However, decades of research have shown that sentence-level measurements do reveal impediments to clarity. As such, these measurements are useful tools for polishing writing that is already sound in its message delivery, organization, and coherence.

THE VALUE OF SENTENCE MEASUREMENTS

In two words: syntax and processing.

Syntax is defined as *the patterns of formation of sentences and phrases from words* (www.dictionary. reference.com, accessed January 26, 2009). In short, this means the way we put words together—following the *rules* of a language—to form sentences. The syntax of English includes the essential relationship of subjects to verbs as well as the relationships of all types of modifiers to what they modify. Consider two sentences, one that uses intact English syntax and one that does not.

Examples

Syntax intact: He wrote the report using the updated data that the audit customer provided.

Syntax not intact: He that the audit customer using updated provided the data wrote the report.

When the syntax is not intact, we cannot make sense of the sentence. In particular, we cannot correctly relate the subjects to their verbs (in the example, *he* and *wrote* as well as *audit customer* and *provided*). We also cannot relate the modifiers to the ideas they modify (in the example, *updated* to *data*).

Processing refers to how the reader makes sense of information as he or she is reading. Intact syntax gets the reader partway there. However, the syntax may be intact but strained; that is, the reader may be forced to hold the syntactical structure in mind for too long before the relationships are clear. Here is our example sentence again, this time with the syntax intact but strained.

> *Example*
>
> Syntax strained: Using the updated data that the audit customer provided, he wrote the report.

In this example, the reader has to hold onto the phrase *using the updated data that the audit customer provided* for a long time before the *user* of the data is revealed (*he*).

These strains of syntax and processing are what the following four measurements aim to expose.

FOUR MEASUREMENTS

Sentence length

Sentence length affects processing. Long sentences introduce so many syntactical components that processing slows down.

A reasonable average sentence length for technical documents ranges from 15 to 20 words. Within that range, the appropriate sentence length for any particular document depends on the characteristics of the target audience. Specifically, these factors should guide your decision about sentence length:

- The target audience's level of understanding: The sentences need to be shorter when the audience is less familiar the content.
- The target audience's familiarity with the terms: The sentences need to be shorter when the audience is unfamiliar with the terms.
- The target audience's attitude: The sentences need to be shorter when the audience has a more negative attitude about the messages.
- The level of distraction in the reading environment: The sentences need to be shorter when the reading environment is physically or psychologically distracting.

Sentence length is easy to measure: you count the words in the sentence. (And yes, you count every word, even *the*, *a*, and *an*.) Your word processor has a tool for counting the words in an individual sentence and for computing the average sentence length for a document section or for an entire document. (Check the Help system if you're not sure how to use this feature.)

Notice that we are focused on average sentence length; we are not focused on any grade-level measurement that your word processor may offer. Such grade-level measurements were created to assess school textbooks, and their use for other types of documents is controversial and unsupported by research. You would be mistaken to assume, for example, that a grade level of 16 means easy reading for every reader with four or more years of college.

The simplest strategy for managing sentence length is to break long sentences into their component parts. Here is an example of this approach.

Example

Original Version: Average Sentence Length = 33.5 words

The Durable Medical Equipment (DME) SuperTrack System tracks the complete history of deliveries, pickups, and repairs of rental equipment and tracks the party to whom equipment has been rented and billed, enabling the department to account for all rental equipment assigned to the customer with billing activities. The system generates key reports on DME equipment location and status, rental agreements, and delivery and billing status and history.

Revision: Average Sentence Length = 14.6 words

The Durable Medical Equipment (DME) SuperTrack System tracks the complete history of rental equipment. Included are deliveries, pickups, and repairs. It also tracks the party to whom equipment has been rented and billed. Thus, the system enables the department to account for all rental equipment assigned to the customer along with billing activities. The system also generates key reports on DME location and status, rental agreements, and delivery and billing status and history.

The next example shows two punctuation strategies for managing sentence length. First, the revision uses a semicolon to link two related ideas. Second, the revision uses bullets to break out some details. Both of these strategies have the same effect on readability as making separate sentences.

Example

Original Version: Average Sentence Length = 29 words

The Shared Service Center (SSC) was established in September 20xx to assume responsibility for various financial, accounting, and treasury functions that had previously been performed by individual hospitals. The Accounts Payable (AP) department, within the SSC, is responsible for processing all disbursements and utilizes SeeClear to image and store invoices and PromptPay to account for and pay invoices.

Revision: Average Sentence Length = 10.5 words (counting the sentence with the semicolon as two sentences, and counting the bullets as separate sentences)

The Shared Service Center (SSC) was established in September 20xx to assume responsibility for various financial, accounting, and treasury functions; these functions had previously been performed by individual hospitals. The Accounts Payable (AP) department, within the SSC, is responsible for processing all disbursements. AP utilizes two core systems:

- SeeClear to image and store invoices
- PromptPay to account for and pay invoices

Subject-to-verb distance

Subjects and verbs want to be close to each other. How close? Research suggests that no more than eight words should separate a subject from its verb. Maintaining such a reasonable distance takes the strain off the syntax.

The strategy shown in the next example is to simply pick up the verb phrase (*were not being enforced*) and place it next to its subject (*the procedures*). The rest of the sentence then falls into place.

Example

Original Version: Distance between Subject and Verb = 10 words

The procedures for controlling access to the secure laboratory and archive areas were not being enforced.

Revision: Distance between Subject and Verb = 0 words

The procedures were not being enforced for controlling access to the secure laboratory and archive areas.

Sometime, simply moving the verb will not work to get the subject and verb closer together. The strategy in the next example is to remove the words between the subject (*materials*) and its verb (*are managed*), creating a separate sentence with those intervening words.

Example

Original Version: Distance between Subject and Verb = 17 words

Materials used in clinical trials, including drugs, vaccines, and non-trial medication supplies as well as required documentation templates, are managed by a dedicated group within the hospital.

Revision: Distance between Subject and Verb = 4 words

Materials used in clinical trials are managed by a dedicated group within the hospital. These materials include drugs, vaccines, and non-trial medication supplies as well as required documentation templates.

Length of introductory elements

An introductory element comprises anything that precedes the main part of a sentence. In grammatical terms, an introductory element may be an introductory word (not a problem for our current discussion), a phrase, or a subordinate (dependent) clause. If these grammatical terms are daunting, just ask yourself where the main idea of the sentence begins: what precedes that main idea is likely an introductory element. Also, you will usually find a comma between the introductory element and the main part of the sentence.

The same metric that applied to subject-to-verb distance applies here: no more than eight words. Again, the measurement aims to avoid straining the syntax.

The example below shows two revision strategies. The first revision picks up the introductory element and moves it to follow the main part of the sentence, altering it just slightly. The second revision shapes the words in the introductory element into a separate sentence.

Examples

Original version: Length of Introductory Element = 18 words

Although significant gains in wellness-program attendance were recorded in November (with 81% attendance) and December (with 75% attendance), attendance averaged only 68% for the year.

Revision A: No Introductory Element

Wellness-program attendance averaged only 68% for the year even though significant gains in attendance were recorded in November (with 81% attendance) and December (with 75% attendance).

Revision B: No Introductory Element

Significant gains in wellness-program attendance were recorded in November (with 81% attendance) and December (with 75% attendance). However, attendance averaged only 68% for the year.

Number of prepositional phrases in a row

First, a definition: prepositions are words that point out the relationship of one idea to another. They show physical or abstract position. Examples include *after, before, by, for, from, of, through, with,* and many more. Another commonly used preposition is *to*. However, *to* also can be part of what we call the infinitive form of verbs: *to report, to explain*, etc. In that case, *to* is not a preposition.

Prepositions introduce prepositional phrases. These are often quite short and are always modifiers of some other idea. The following sentence contains three prepositional phrases: *During* Q1 20xx, departments began implementing procedures *for* reducing incidents *of* medical errors.

Syntax is strained when four or more prepositional phrases occur in a row. The reader must strain to remember how the phrases relate to the ideas they modify. Furthermore, such sentences sound choppy.

The strategy in the following example is to convert some of the phrases into direct modifiers.

Examples

Original Version: Prepositional Phrases in a Row = 5 phrases

Weaknesses in the process led to variations in how outcomes of critical events were documented in the database.

Revision: Prepositional Phrases in a Row = 3 phrases

Process weaknesses led to variations in how critical-event outcomes were documented in the database.

COMBINED IMPACT OF SENTENCE MEASUREMENTS

The advantage of using these measurements is their objectivity. They are outside of style or preference. You may apply them to your own writing, or you may use them to help other writers improve their writing.

Here is a final example that addresses all four measurements. The result demonstrates their power.

Examples

Original Version

The One-Day-Surgery Patient Handbook provides guidance to patients admitted to the Surgery Center for procedures requiring a stay of less than 24 hours. The Handbook, published on an annual basis by the Customer-Relations Department with review by physicians and nurses, covers issues such as the surgery-center staff, facilities, visitors, privacy, and patients' rights. Depending on the type of surgery for which the patient has been admitted and the preference of the physician, the Handbook may be supplemented with an information sheet covering specific issues related to the treatment of the patient.

Revision

The One-Day-Surgery Patient Handbook provides guidance to Surgery-Center patients admitted for procedures requiring a less-than-24-hour stay. The Handbook covers issues such as the surgery-center staff, facilities, visitors, privacy, and patients' rights. It is published annually by the Customer-Relations Department and reviewed by nurses and physicians. A supplemental information sheet may be provided on issues specific to the patient's treatment. Such a supplement is included depending on the type of surgery and the physician's preference.

You're ready to try counting your way to clearer sentences. You know that these measurements can't solve every writing problem. But when you applied them to your draft, lots of sentences proved much easier to read.

Chapter Three:
Managing Technical Content

Your chief audit executive has asked you to write up a technical issue so "anyone can understand it." But how do you do that? Your readers are smart and well educated, but their technical specialties vary. The issue is complex, and you're struggling to make it understandable without misrepresenting it.

This chapter describes an approach to the challenge of writing for technically-diverse readerships. Specifically, it promotes layering and navigation. Then, it provides advice about how to adjust various sections of a document for less-technical and more-technical readers. Finally, it addresses the sometimes vexing mechanics of handling abbreviations.

LAYERING AND NAVIGATION

You might think that the best way to address a diverse readership is to compromise on the level of technicality, that is, to hit some middle level of complexity. However, such a compromise satisfies neither type of reader: it stresses the less-technical readers and under-serves the more-technical ones.

A combination of layering and navigation is the solution to the challenges of a technically-diverse readership. Layering and navigation empower the readers to make decisions about what to read and what not to read.

Layering

When you layer the document, you adjust different sections of the document to suit different readers: some sections are for the less-technical readers, and some are for the more-technical ones. You layer the document by carefully dividing the content, with a realistic eye to what each readership segment wants and needs.

- The overall structure of the document can be layered. For example, including an executive summary in a report is a kind of layering; so is the inclusion of appendices.
- The information within each section of the document can be layered. When you do so, including navigation strategies supports the layering.

Navigation

Navigation enables readers to find their way in a layered document. In addition, navigation gives readers permission to bypass the parts of the document that are not useful to them. Navigation is created by using layout, graphic cues, and wording to direct the readers' attention.

DOCUMENT SECTIONS AIMED AT LESS-TECHNICAL READERS

For document sections aimed at less-technical readers, the following strategies are effective.

Explanations or reminders of underlying concepts

Less-technical readers need to understand—or to be reminded about—the concepts that underlie the ideas. Furthermore, when you anchor these concepts to what these readers already know, you enable the readers to understand the new ideas and information you are presenting. This writing principle is called *known-new.* For example, you might write, *Following the implementation of HIPAA, the hospital upgraded its information technology (IT) systems to better protect patient information* [known concepts for the reader]. *However, increasing sophistication in identity-theft has caused the hospital's IT department to install automated intrusion-detection software* [new information for the reader]. *This audit assessed the effectiveness of that software installation* [new information for the reader].

Fewer details

Some writers believe they can help less-technical readers by providing more details. These writers try to raise the understanding of less-technical readers to the writer's own level of understanding.

However, such an approach is mistaken. Less-technical readers know that the details are important to someone, and they may even feel obliged to try to understand. But the effort is out of proportion to the rewards. The less-technical reader gets lost, gets discouraged, or—the worst case—misunderstands. Less-technical readers have difficulty seeing what is relevant and grasping which details are significant.

Less-technical readers need fewer details, not more. They need the high-level concepts based on the details, not the details themselves. Their understanding may be enhanced by pertinent details in specific areas, but they do not need to know everything that you know. Rather, they need you to use your technical level of understanding to interpret the details for them. (See *Part One, Chapter Three: Solving the Goldilocks Dilemma* for more on handling details.)

Avoidance or definitions of technical terms

The technically correct term may be baffling for less-technical readers. It may stymie them, or they may misunderstand it.

One approach is to avoid using technical terms in the document sections aimed at the less-technical readers. For example, say you call your audit methodology COBRA, which stands for COSO-based Risk Auditing. Your reader needs a description of your audit methodology, namely, that you audit the highest risks using a well-established method for identifying risks; however, your reader may never need to know your pet name for this methodology. In fact, including that name may introduce a distraction—what we call noise—into the communication.

Another approach—when less-technical readers do need to understand a technical term—is to define the term. There are three ways to do so: by embedding the definition, by providing the definition elsewhere, and—if the document will be read electronically—by providing the definition in a mouse rollover.

You may embed a definition within parentheses, which serve as a graphic cue, or you may embed it in a separate sentence, which calls attention to the definition through wording. Here are examples of embedded definitions.

Examples

Definition embedded with parentheses

Cardiac rehabilitation may be provided as an incident to benefit (a benefit requiring the physician to see the patient periodically but not to perform a personal professional service each time the patient attends rehabilitation).

Definition embedded as a separate sentence

Cardiac rehabilitation may be provided as what is called an incident to benefit. Such a benefit requires the physician to see the patient periodically but not to perform a personal professional service each time the patient attends rehabilitation.

You may provide the definition elsewhere, for example, in a glossary or a footnote. The graphic cue for the footnote is, of course, the superscript number; a graphic cue for a glossary term could be italics or underlining. However, footnote and glossary definitions slow down the reader, so use this approach when the primary readership is more technical and the secondary readership is less technical.

For an electronic document, you may use a mouse rollover (the definition pops up when the cursor rests over the term) or a hyperlink. Either way, a graphic cue should signal the reader that a definition is available.

Shorter sentences

Less-technical readers need shorter sentences, with the information parceled out in manageable segments. For document sections aimed at less-technical readers, strive for an average sentence length around 15 words. (See *Part Two, Chapter Two: Using Sentence Measurements to Improve Clarity* for more on sentence length.)

DOCUMENT SECTIONS AIMED AT MORE-TECHNICAL READERS

For document sections aimed at more-technical readers, the following strategies are effective.

More details

More-technical readers want and need details, and they want to see how you reached conclusions based on those details. They will scrutinize the quality of the information and assess your credibility as an honest reporter of the details. Explanations or reminders of underlying principles, however, generally get in the way of fluid reading for more-technical readers. (See *Part One, Chapter Three: Solving the Goldilocks Dilemma* for more on handling levels of detail.)

Technical terms

Technical terms are useful—even essential—for more-technical readers. Such terms ease the reading; they communicate in a short-hand, precise way. Furthermore, with this readership, the absence of the technically-correct term may reduce your credibility as the writer.

Longer sentences

More-technical readers can stand longer sentences because these readers are familiar with the concepts. An average sentence length up to 25 words will generally not impede their reading. They can follow the line of thought and see the relationship of ideas.

NAVIGATION STRATEGIES

Headings, sidebars, and appendices can provide useful navigation for both less-technical and more-technical readers.

Headings

All readers appreciate headings that identify what will follow. In general, the more informative the heading, the more useful it will be for the reader. Consider, for example, the limited utility of the heading *Background* versus the more useful *Previous initiatives to reduce medication errors*. Or, compare the heading *Process description* to the heading *Description of intake process*.

Sidebars

A sidebar is text that is visually separated from the main text; it may be shaded or boxed, and it may be placed so that the main text wraps around it. The visual separation gives the reader permission to skip the information. Coupled with a sidebar heading that tells what's in the box, a sidebar provides effective navigation for diverse readerships.

- For less-technical readers, sidebars may contain explanations of basic concepts, background information, or call-outs that highlight key points in the main text.
- For more-technical readers, sidebars may provide details, expanded discussions, methodology, or reference information.

Appendices

Consider placing more-technical information in an appendix when the material is too extensive for a footnote or sidebar. Turning to (or hyperlinking to) an appendix slows the reading, so appendices are most useful when the less-technical readers are the primary readers of the document; the more-technical readers will be willing to do the work of navigating to the appendix.

Beware of two pitfalls in creating an appendix: burying essential information there, and failing to be selective. An appendix should be as carefully constructed as the rest of the document. If essential information is buried in an appendix, abstract that information into the main text. And if the appendix contains extraneous information, excise that information.

HOW TO HANDLE ABBREVIATIONS

We love the abbreviations we know, but we hate the ones we don't know. (In the following discussion, the word *abbreviation* refers to both abbreviations and acronyms. An abbreviation is a shortened form, usually using the first letters of the words being shortened. For example, the United States is referred to as the US. An acronym is an abbreviation pronounced as a word. For example, *SARS* is an acronym.)

Abbreviations are common in technical documents because technical content contains strings of specialized terms. Consider how cumbersome it would be to repeatedly write *magnetic resonance imaging* instead of *MRI*. Furthermore, an abbreviation rapidly becomes the name for the entire concept, system, or project it represents.

The convention for handling an abbreviation is to define it the first time you use it, stating the full term followed by the abbreviation in parentheses, like this: *magnetic resonance imaging (MRI)*. Once you have done so, you are theoretically free to use the abbreviation in the rest of the document. This is called defining the abbreviation on first mention. But the first-mention approach is fraught with real-world problems:

- The references are too far apart. No reader will remember what the abbreviation means if you introduce it on page 2 but do not use it again until page 20. Repeat the full definition with the abbreviation, or drop the abbreviation entirely.
- There are too many abbreviations. Confusion builds when you use too many abbreviations in proximity. Avoid abbreviations for terms you repeat least often, reserving the abbreviations for the most common two or three.
- Nobody knows what the abbreviation stands for anymore. Sometimes, the terms behind the abbreviation have been forgotten, even though the readers still know what the abbreviation means. For example, most people probably have to think twice to define the acronym *HIPAA*. When the readers know the abbreviation better than its definition, present the abbreviation first and the definition second, like this: *HIPAA (Health Insurance Portability and Accountability Act)*.

Finally, select the article *a* or the article *an* before an abbreviation based on the sound, not the spelling. For example, write *a SARS epidemic* but *an MRI study*. (We pronounce *MRI* starting with the vowel sound *eh*, as in *em*, so the article *an* is correct.)

You've considered your readership and decided how to layer the document for your more-technical and less-technical readers. Your document has informative headings, some embedded definitions, three helpful sidebars, a short glossary, and two appendices. (And you've kept those abbreviations under control!) Your readers are delighted, and your chief audit executive's aim of helping everyone understand has been achieved.

You've completed an audit with important findings—not so significant that the executives will be knocking on the audit customer's door, but serious enough nonetheless—and you've just drafted the audit report. You want your audit customer to get the message: the problems you've found need to be corrected, and the causes of those problems need to be addressed. Throughout this audit, you've worked diligently to keep the audit customer informed; in particular, you've shared your findings worksheets, so the report will contain no surprises.

But you're struggling with the tone of this report. You've trying to find the right balance, not too harsh and not too mild. Also, you need to match the tone of the writing to the severity of the issues, to support the facts by the way you use the words. You want to gain the audit customer's support, and you'd like to do so without creating defensiveness.

This chapter describes three understandings that can help you control tone: what tone is, how to adjust it, and how to avoid tonal problems.

WHAT TONE IS

When you speak, you use more than words to fully communicate the message. Specifically, you incorporate facial expressions and body language; in addition, you alter the way your voice sounds— what is called your tone of voice. Consider the following sentence: *What did you do yesterday?* By emphasizing different words in the sentence, you affect its meaning. *What DID you do yesterday?* conveys something quite different from *What did YOU do yesterday?*

However, writing lacks the communication components of facial expression, body language, and tone of voice. Words alone convey the message. Thus, when we refer to the tone of writing, we are referring to the often subtle messages that readers take from how we select and use words.

HOW TO ADJUST TONE

Four factors affect tone in writing. By managing these, you can control the tone:

- Connotation
- Placement of negation
- Proportion and sequence of negative and positive information
- Negative and positive projection

The content of internal audit messages is usually negative, so these four factors are crucial in communicating how relatively negative, severe, and significant the audit issues are.

Connotation

Words have denotation and connotation. Denotation is the meaning or definition of the word; it is the agreed-upon dictionary definition. Connotation is the subtle emotional reference or shading of the word, and connotation evokes a reaction in the reader that goes beyond meaning.

Some words have stronger connotations than others. For example, words such as *the* (the definite article); *of, in, over, for,* and so forth (prepositions); and *am, are, is* (forms of the verb *to be*) have no connotation. They are neutral and evoke no response in the reader. On the other hand, some words— curse words and racially or ethnically derogatory terms, for example—have such negative connotations that they are not used in writing (or aloud) in civil communication. Between the two extremes are words that can evoke most human emotions.

Unlike the denotation of a word, its connotation can vary widely from individual to individual. Each person develops his or her own connotations for words, based on exposure to the words. Ask a group of people to place a series of negative terms in order based on the degree of negativity, and the results will vary. Moreover, the variety of connotations will increase the more regionally, socially, temperamentally, or linguistically diverse the group is.

In fact, the variations are particularly interesting when the group includes second-language speakers. For those who speak more than one language, the word's first-language connotation influences the connotation of the translated word. For example, asked to rank *mad, angry, irate,* and *furious,* many second-language speakers of American English place *mad* above *irate* and *furious,* apparently owing to the connotation of *insanity* for *mad*—a connotation no longer present for most first-language American English speakers.

Understanding connotation is the starting point for understanding how to control the tone of your writing. Consider these four ways of expressing almost the same idea.

Examples

Version A: The absence of training limited the employees' understanding of the process.

Version B: Lack of training led to employees misunderstanding the process.

Version C: Employees were not trained, so they were uninformed about the process.

Version D: Failure to train employees resulted in their ignorance of the process.

Sometimes the connotations differ subtly: Is *absence of training* harsher or milder than *lack of training*? Is it worse to *misunderstand* or to be *uninformed*? And sometimes the connotation differences are not subtle: Wouldn't most of us agree that *failure* and *ignorance* are likely to raise the readers' blood pressure?

Placement of negation

In English, ideas can be negated by directly negating nouns and verbs (using *no* and *not*), negating adjectives by using prefixes (such as *non*, *in*, and *un*), and using words that contain the negation. Consider the way the negation is created in the following sentences.

Examples

Direct negation of the noun: No documentation existed for the patient transfers.

Direct negation of the verb: Documentation did not exist for the patient transfers.

Negation of the adjective using the prefix *non*: Documentation was nonexistent for the patient transfers.

Negation using a negative word (absent): Documentation was absent for the patient transfers.

As demonstrated for connotation, the tonal shifts can be subtle. Starting a sentence with the word *no* is potent, but so is attaching the prefix *non* to the word *existent*. Consider also that a series of sentences all beginning with *no* will compound the negativity.

Proportion and sequence of negative and positive information

Connotation and negation focus on individual words. However, readers also infer tone from whether there is a mix of negative and positive information—what we call proportion—and the sequencing of this information. Consider the proportion and sequence in the following examples.

Examples

Version A: The organization has improved expense reporting by providing online guidance and user-friendly tools for reporting. Expense reports did, however, lack some documentation and were not always consistently reviewed.

Version B: Executive expense reports did not include all required documentation, and expense reviews were not being consistently conducted as required. The organization has, however, made efforts to improve reporting with online guidance and tools.

In Version A, 16 words describe the positive aspects of the activity—and these words come first—while 13 words describe the negative aspects. In contrast, in Version B, 14 words describe the positive aspects—and these words come last—while 19 words describe the negative aspects. As a result, the first example is noticeably more positive than the second, and the messages communicated are different.

Negative and positive projection

The final tone factor is projection, specifically, how effects are projected. They may be projected as the negative effects of failing to resolve causes—called negative projection—or as the positive effects of successfully resolving causes—called positive projection. Consider the projection in the following examples.

> *Examples*
>
> Negative projection: Failure to conduct employee performance reviews on a timely basis increases employee dissatisfaction and decreases overall morale.
>
> Positive projection: Conducting employee performance reviews on a timely basis increases employee satisfaction and overall morale.

Many times, your audit report will communicate findings that range in severity. While positive projection is inappropriate for significant or severe findings, it is effective for toning down less severe ones. If you incorporate positive projection in the less severe findings, you help your readers see the relative significance of the findings. Furthermore, your audit customer will perceive a measure of balance in your report, which in itself can be persuasive.

HOW TO AVOID TONE PROBLEMS

How, then, can you avoid tone problems?

One strategy is to match tone to severity. Do your audit findings—regardless of their relative severity—use the same degree of negative wording, present the same proportion of negative and positive information (or present negative information only), and project the effects always as negative ones? If so, the reader may get the impression that all findings are equally severe or significant, when that is rarely the case. Try using the four factors to adjust the tone to match the severity.

A second strategy is to realize that some words are *fighting words* and to avoid them altogether. They raise emotional defenses in a reader. Words with strong negative connotations—*failure, incompetence, negligence, ignorance*, and many more—can create so much hostility in the reader that the reader cannot attend to the message. Try avoiding the fighting words that make readers defensive.

A third strategy is to pay attention to how readers react to particular sentences. If your reader seems to be over-reacting to an issue, try to determine the exact words that are troubling the reader. Perhaps the reader is bringing a different connotation to those words, and perhaps you can revise without losing meaning.

Fortunately for you, a more experienced colleague provided advice about how to control tone. The result was a report that communicated the messages fully and fairly. The audit customer was satisfied that the audit report reflected what the auditor had been communicating all along.

Chapter Five:
Grappling with Grammar

Your boss is a stickler for "good grammar." You test your grammar to see if it sounds right, which usually works. But sometimes your boss finds a grammar error, and you can't see what's wrong. You haven't studied grammar in a while, and when you look at a grammar book, the terms are confusing.

This chapter aims to bridge the gap between relying on what sounds right and developing a deep understanding of grammar. It covers some common errors American English writers make in pronoun use, sentence structure, agreement, and punctuation. It also offers advice about passive voice.

DEFINITION, PLEASE

Contrary to what many think, grammar is not a set of rules superimposed on a language. Rather, grammar is what enables a language user to make statements that other users of the same language can understand. Grammar is a brain-based machine for combining words in meaningful ways.

If you are a first-language user of a language—if you learned it from birth or at a young age—your grammar is automatic. You speak without thinking about subjects, verbs, objects, tenses, agreement, and the other elements we associate with the word *grammar*, and others understand you.

The brain is wonderfully adapted to do this. In fact, research demonstrates that when the developing brain learns a language, neurological pathways are actually altered. We might say that your first language is installed *hardware*.

CORRECTNESS AND BAD GRAMMAR

For three reasons, that hardware might not measure up to your boss's expectations: installed variations, long sentences, and the scrutiny placed on writing.

Your installed grammar may be what linguists call nonstandard. That is, you may have learned a variation of what a society considers correct. If you have installed variations, testing what sounds right may yield *bad* grammar. Keep in mind, though, that the notion of correctness is new in the history of language and is anathema to linguists, who agree that all variations are equal as long as they enable communication. The notion of correctness comes with the leveling effects of the printing press and then of mass media.

Nonstandard grammar is common, and almost everyone has some installed variations. For example, the *correct* response to *Who's there?* is *It's I*. Most American English speakers, though, say *It's me*.

Long sentences are another source of problems. Such sentences may push elements so far apart that you can no longer hear an error. For example, the following sentence may sound right: *Analysis* conducted on the outcomes of audits completed during the first and second quarters have shown an increase in compliance issues. However, removing the words between *analysis* and *have shown* highlights the error: *have shown* should be *has shown*.

Finally, writing gets more scrutiny than speech. Most of us make errors in speech, and listeners gloss over these, if they even catch them. Readers, however, reread and ponder. Writing invites closer examination.

With all this in mind, you know your boss is looking for better grammar, that is, standard American English. Following are some common errors with suggestions for recognizing and correcting them.

PRONOUN-USE ERRORS

I, *me*, and *myself* are frequently misused. We call these the first-person singular personal pronouns. In English, personal pronouns fall into categories based on what the pronoun does in the sentence. Specifically, pronouns may be subjects (*I*) or objects (*me*). Additionally, reflexive pronouns (*myself*) serve as objects when the subject and the object are the same person.

First-language English users usually pick the right subject pronoun. However, one common installed variation is to substitute the object pronoun. If you make this error, you'll need to teach yourself the standard subject pronouns and when to use them. Here is an example of subject-pronoun misuse.

> *Example*
>
> Incorrect: Him and me received the email.
>
> Correct: He and I received the email.

First-language English users pick the right pronoun in the object position if the pronoun is alone. However, once the pronoun is not alone, errors are more common. Here are examples of object-pronoun use and misuse.

> *Example*
>
> Correct: He sent the email to me.
>
> Incorrect: He sent the email to James and I.
>
> Correct: He sent the email to James and me.

Finally, errors often occur with the reflexive pronouns, the ones with -self or -selves attached. Here are examples of reflexive pronoun use and misuse.

> *Example*
>
> Correct: I sent a copy of the email to myself.
>
> Incorrect: You should send a copy of the email to myself.
>
> Correct: You should send a copy of the email to me.

SENTENCE-STRUCTURE ERRORS

Two common sentence-structure errors are modifier errors and lack of parallel structure.

A modifier is a word or phrase that alters the meaning of another word. In the following sentence, *annual* is a modifier, altering the meaning of *report*, and *audit* is a modifier, altering the meaning of *committee*: *The annual report to the audit committee was issued in January.*

In English, a modifier needs to be as close as possible to what it modifies, otherwise the sentence is unclear. One common error occurs when a modifying phrase starts a sentence. Here is an example of such a modifier problem.

> *Example*
>
> Incorrect: While auditing environmental safety, unlabeled 55-gallon drums were found in the storage area.
>
> Correct: While auditing environmental safety, we found unlabeled 55-gallon drums in the storage area.

In the incorrect version, the phrase *While auditing environmental safety* modifies *unlabeled 55-gallon drums*. Thus, the sentence literally says that the drums performed the audit. Many revisions are possible; the revision shown retains the modifying phrase and inserts *we* to correct the error.

Another common modifier problem occurs with words like *only*, *even*, and *almost*. Here is an example of such a problem.

> *Example*
>
> Incorrect: Employees only conducted reviews if discrepancies were found.
>
> Correct: Employees conducted reviews only if discrepancies were found.

In the incorrect version, *only* modifies *conducted reviews*, but it should modify the *if* condition. The revision corrects the error by placing *only* next to *if*.

Lack of parallel structure is another sentence-structure error. Parallel structure is lacking when related elements do not match grammatically. This error is most common in lists, including bulleted ones. Here is an example of a parallel-structure problem.

> *Example*
>
> Incorrect: Changes were made to improve communications, assign accountability, and adverse-event reporting.
>
> Correct: Changes were made to improve communications, assign accountability, and ensure adverse-event reporting.

In the incorrect version, *improve* and *assign* are both verbs, but *adverse-event reporting* is not. The revision solves the problem by inserting the verb *ensure*.

AGREEMENT ERRORS

Two types of agreement are standard in English: agreement of a verb with its subject and agreement of a pronoun with the word it stands for (called its antecedent).

Agreement of verbs and subjects

When a verb is close to its subject, most first-language English users automatically make the verb agree. However, once the verb and subject get pushed apart, it's harder to hear the agreement. Here is an example of lack of agreement.

> *Example*
>
> Incorrect: Analysis conducted on the outcomes of audits completed during the first and second quarters have shown an increase in compliance issues.
>
> Correct: Analysis conducted on the outcomes of audits completed during the first and second quarters has shown an increase in compliance issues.
>
> Also correct: Analysis was conducted on the outcomes of audits completed during the first and second quarters. This analysis has shown an increase in compliance issues.

In the incorrect version, the verb *have shown* does not agree with its subject, *analysis*. The revision corrects the agreement problem by changing *have* to *has*.

To help avoid this problem—and to increase readability—you should keep the verbs no more than eight words from their subjects. Sometimes, applying this advice calls for breaking the sentence (as shown in the second revision above). (See *Part Two, Chapter Two: Using Sentence Measurements to Improve Clarity* for more on subject-to-verb distance.)

Other verb-to-subject agreement errors occur when subjects are complex, especially with subjects that are sometimes plural and other times singular. These include words such as *staff*, *committee*, and *faculty*. When these words refer to the group as a unit, they are singular, but when they refer to the group as a collection of individuals, they are plural. Here are examples of complex agreement problems.

> *Examples*
>
> Incorrect: The staff meet on Monday mornings.
>
> Correct: The staff meets on Monday mornings.
>
> Incorrect: The staff holds differing professional designations.
>
> Correct: The staff hold differing professional designations.

In the first incorrect sentence and its revision, *staff* is a unit and so is singular; in the second incorrect sentence and its revision, *staff* is a collection of individuals and so is plural.

Finally, verb-to-subject agreement can be confusing when the subject includes *or* or *nor*, in which case the verb agrees with the final part of the subject. Here is an example of agreement with *or*.

> *Example*
>
> Incorrect: Either the procedures or the report were altered.
>
> Correct: Either the procedures or the report was altered.

In the incorrect version, the verb, *were*, agrees with *procedures* instead of agreeing with *report* (as corrected in the revision).

Agreement of pronouns and antecedents

Agreement of pronouns and antecedents is usually automatic for first-language English users, with plurals matching plurals and singulars matching singulars. Here is an example of lack of pronoun agreement.

> *Example*
>
> Incorrect: A total of 12 employees had not updated his passwords.
>
> Correct: A total of 12 employees had not updated their passwords.

However, English distinguishes gender in only one set of personal pronouns: the third-person singular ones. Writers trying to eliminate gender bias are challenged to select the correct pronoun to match a singular third-person noun: *Each employee must update his security clearance annually.* Unless all employees are male, this sentence is biased.

Several solutions are possible. One is using the plural pronoun, even though it will disagree; this is the solution we hear most often in speech: *Each employee must update their security clearance annually.* Another is writing *his/her*. However, this solution is unpronounceable and cumbersome if repeated. A better solution is making the antecedent plural: *Employees must update their security clearances annually.* Another good solution is rewriting to eliminate the pronoun: *Each employee must annually file an updated security clearance.*

PUNCTUATION ERRORS

Punctuation is not installed as grammar is because we do not speak it. Thus, even if you have few installed variations, punctuation can be puzzling. Moreover, education has not always kept pace with punctuation changes. As a result, many of us learned outmoded punctuation conventions.

Of the possible punctuation errors, two stand out: the comma splice and the omission of the serial comma.

Comma splice

A comma splice occurs when you use a comma to splice together two complete, independent sentences. This error often occurs when the second sentence begins with *however*. Here is an example of such an error with several ways to correct it.

Example

Incorrect: Procedures were updated, however, the nursing supervisors were not trained on them.

Correct: Procedures were updated; however, the nursing supervisors were not trained on them.

Also correct: Procedures were updated. However, the nursing supervisors were not trained on them.

Also correct: Procedures were updated, but the nursing supervisors were not trained on them.

In the incorrect version, a complete sentence comes both before and after *however*. Current American-English punctuation allows only the following words (called coordinate conjunctions) after a comma to join two complete, independent sentences: *and, but, or, for, nor, yet, so.* The revisions correct the problem by substituting either a semicolon or a period for the comma or by changing *however* to *but* and retaining the comma.

Serial comma

The serial comma is the source of more debate than is any other punctuation mark. The serial comma is the one before *and* (or *or*) in a series. In the following sentence, the serial comma is the one after *training*: *Improvements are necessary in documentation, training, and monitoring.* Many of us were taught to omit this comma, some were taught it was optional, and some were taught to use it always. Those last are the fortunate ones because including the serial comma is the current American-English convention for technical and business writing.

Variations

Here's a final note on punctuation conventions: they vary not only from language to language but also among different countries using what we consider to be the same language. In particular, British-English and American-English punctuation conventions differ. The country you are in or the one where your organization is based will dictate which conventions you follow.

PASSIVE VOICE

Both active voice and passive voice are grammatically correct. Also, voice—while a characteristic of verbs—is not the same as tense. The verb uses active voice when the subject of the verb carries out the action; the verb uses passive voice when the subject of the verb is the person or thing acted upon. In general, active voice yields shorter, more energetic sentences.

Passive voice, however, has important uses. It emphasizes the person or thing acted upon, and such emphasis may be appropriate. Furthermore, passive voice can soften the tone. Here are examples of active voice and passive voice.

Examples

Active voice: Management had not cancelled the inactive passwords.

Passive voice: The inactive passwords had not been cancelled.

Now when your boss corrects your grammar, you'll try to identify a theme. Perhaps you have nonstandard installed variations in grammar; in that case, you'll have work to do to start using standard grammar. Perhaps you can see the errors better if you write shorter sentences. Or perhaps you need to acknowledge that written communications—and especially reports—get more scrutiny than speech and so require more attention to the details of grammar.

Chapter Six:
Proofreading

Once again, you've issued what you believed was a well-organized, well-written audit report only to discover that it is tarnished by typographical errors. The heading of the report had the wrong date in it. The numbering for one of the graphics didn't match its reference in the report. "Result sin" incorrectly appeared in place of "results in." And—perhaps worst of all—the CFOs last name, "Pace," was misspelled as "Place." How can you make sure that these kinds of errors don't continue to turn up in your reports?

This chapter distinguishes proofreading from editing and copyediting—two activities that should precede proofreading. The chapter also makes the case for proofreading as a crucial step in assuring writing quality, even in an email and text-message culture. Finally, the chapter provides proven strategies for developing proofreading proficiency and for helping writers and those who review their writing to ensure polished final documents.

DEFINITION, PLEASE

Lots of writers use the word *proofreading* to refer to anything that they and others do to a document once it's written. However, proofreading has a narrower meaning, and understanding how it differs from editing and from what we call *copyediting* can help you ensure final-document quality.

- Editing is the activity of revising your or someone else's writing, including changing the organization, content, level of detail, sentence structure, wording, tone, and so forth.
- Copyediting is the activity of revising your or someone else's writing leaving the writing essentially intact while making it more concise, resolving unclear syntax, and correcting errors in grammar and punctuation.
- Proofreading is literally test reading: checking the accuracy of references external to the document, assuring the consistency of format and references within the document, and correcting typographical errors.

Editing, copyediting, and proofreading all contribute to writing quality, but few writers can perform these tasks simultaneously. Rather, they should be done sequentially. Even when someone else will review your writing, you should edit, copyedit, and proofread, providing the reviewer with the best document that you can. Doing so makes the reviewer's task easier and also usually prompts fewer changes.

The specific areas of concern for proofreading are accuracy, consistency, and correction.

Accuracy

- Of references external to the document, including citations of external regulations and internal policies as well as references to related documents
- Of titles and names, including those of organizations, departments, systems, locations, and people
- Of dates, including those for the audit period and the reporting

Consistency

- Of format against document standards, including section titles and their organization
- Of format within the document, for example, styles for heading levels, for text, and for tables and graphics
- Of cross-references within the document, for example, references from the text to tables, figures, graphics, and appendices

Correction

- Of typographical errors, including word substitutions, transpositions, and omissions as well as misspellings

You can see how, with all of these issues to attend to, proofreading should be a separate step in the writing process: the final step before a document is published.

WHY IT MATTERS

Text does not need to be perfect to be understood. In fact, you may have seen examples of how it is possible to read words with the inside vowels missing: *Ths is an exmple of how we prcss wrds.*

In fact, most of the time, proofreading errors do not render the text incomprehensible. So, since you can read deficient spelling and supply missing words, why should you worry about such errors? The answer is two-fold:

- Distraction: Errors slow readers down and distract them from the messages. For an instant, the reader must focus on the writing itself, rather than on the message being delivered.
- Reputation: Proofreading errors can justifiably cause your reader to question the care you took with the audit itself, that is, to question your testing and the way you reached your conclusions and recommendations. Furthermore, audit-report readers may already be resistant to or skeptical about your messages. Errors may give such readers an opening to question your work overall.

In the end, the quality of your audit-report product should reflect your professionalism. A carefully proofread, polished document should be one of your goals as an audit professional.

What about less formal documents, like email? Most email readers will forgive an occasional misused word, grammatical or punctuation error, or even a misspelling (although there is less justification for such an error). Keep in mind, however, that our writing conventions—standardized spelling, complete sentences, punctuation, capitalization—evolved to make writing easier to read. Thus, the few minutes it takes to proof an email will pay off in supporting your message as well as your professionalism.

PROOFREADING STRATEGIES

We know that some of us are better at proofreading than are others. I once had a colleague who could look at a page of text and instantly pick out a spelling error. (She was, in fact, a spelling-bee champ.) She literally had an eye for words: she tested spelling by how the words looked, not by how they sounded. Ask yourself this question: When you need to look up a phone number, do you remember it by repeating it to yourself or by seeing it in your mind's eye? If you remember by repeating, you likely are an auditory speller, and you likely have a harder time with spelling—and with proofreading in general—than do those who are visual spellers.

Still, anyone can improve his or her proficiency as a proofreader by using some basic strategies. These include attending to timing, the environment, your process and your use of automated tools.

Timing

One of the best strategies for proficient proofreading is to allow time between when you copyedit and you proofread. Leaving a document over to the next day—or better yet several days hence—significantly increases your ability to catch errors.

Perhaps you cannot build that time into your schedule. If so, even a few minutes' break—time to take your eyes off the computer screen, stretch, or do some other task—helps to break your connection with the text. You are more likely to see an error and not to see what is not actually there.

Another timing strategy is to know when you are at your best for proofreading. Perhaps it's first thing in the morning, when you may feel less distracted or hurried and when your office environment may be quieter. Or maybe you're sharpest later in the day, when the meetings are done and things are winding down. Knowing your own best times and scheduling your proofreading accordingly will improve your likelihood of success.

The environment

Changing the environment of the proofreading also can help.

- Change the way the text looks. Printing the text often makes errors easier to see. For example, checking for consistency is often easier with a paper copy. In addition, some proofreaders prefer to hand-mark changes and input them later. But if you don't want to use paper in this way, you can change the way the text looks by adjusting the percentage view (the zoom) on the screen. Doing so often is sufficient to allow you to see the text differently and to proofread more proficiently.
- Relocate yourself. You may find that taking your laptop to a different place (say, an empty conference room) gives you a different view of the text. Some proofreaders reserve a particular location for doing nothing but proofreading. The location becomes a physical cue for the kind of concentration that proofreading requires.

An effective process

Start off by assuming two things.

- Assume that everything that can possibly be wrong with the document probably will be wrong with the document. This is the glass-half-empty pessimism that makes for a good proofreader. Assume that the dates will be wrong, the names will be misspelled, and every sentence will be missing a word or contain an embarrassing word substitution. Optimists, who think they will just give it one more look, won't find nearly as many of the problems as will pessimists.
- Assume that every time you touch the document, you will introduce another error. You will put your hands on the keyboard to fix a simple error and will inadvertently mess up something else. It happens all the time.

Then, use some or all of the following strategies to improve your proofreading proficiency:

- Go slower than your normal reading speed. On screen, drag the cursor under the text, line by line. On paper, use a ruler or blank sheet of paper on a paper copy to underline the text line by line.
- Break up the proofreading task, making multiple passes through the document. For example, check the format first; then proofread all the headings, followed by the cross-references for figures and tables and lastly the text itself.
- When you find an error, look around in the neighborhood of the error. Errors often are clustered. Furthermore, you need to resist the notion that proofreading is a kind of treasure hunt, with one error allotted per sentence or paragraph or page.
- Always check not only the change you just made but the text surrounding the change, to ensure you have not introduced another error.
- Make a hot list. The list should include the names (departments, organizations, systems, job titles) and the abbreviations and acronyms contained in the document. Be sure your hot list is accurate—check with reliable sources, if need be—and then use the hot list to check for accuracy throughout the document. This will help you avoid, for example, calling a department *Global Vendor Assessment and Procurement* in one place and *Global Procurement and Vendor Assessment* somewhere else. (If you find this unlikely, I can testify to seeing internal audit functions name themselves two different ways in the same document.)
- Be particularly careful about certain parts of the text that are more likely to contain errors. Specifically, we tend not to read section titles and headings carefully, we tend to let out eyes glide over numeric information, and we often miss errors in numbered lists.
- For hand-marked text, consider proofreading with a partner when checking the *live* text against the *dead* hand-marked text. You are working together to check that all the hand-marked changes have been picked up in the *live* text.

The use of automated tools

Spell check is the most obvious automated proofreading tool. It's worthwhile to actively run the spell check before you close the document, even if you have the spelling-error notation turned on (the red squiggly underscore). However, as many have found to their chagrin, spell check cannot check context, so it cannot reveal word substitutions, such as *form* for *from* or *then* for *than*.

One way to guard against your most common word substitutions is to use the *Find* function in your word processor. Keep a list of your most frequent substitutions, and use the *Find* function to check for inappropriate uses. (Do not, however, engage the automatic correction for word substitutions; you still want to control such corrections.)

Style check also may seem like a worthwhile automated tool. However, language is complex, and automated style checking suffers from errors of omission and of commission: it misses many errors and it marks errors where none exist. If you use it, be sure you understand its limitations.

Finally, your word processor's ability to record input from others within the document (to *track changes*) is a useful tool for collaborative editing, copyediting and proofreading. However, input in one file from multiple reviewers, editors and proofreaders can be overwhelming, so use this tool carefully.

You're determined to ensure your reports have the quality and polish that reflects your overall professionalism. You'll make proofreading a separate step in the writing process and practice strategies to increase your proficiency. The payoff will be your ability to deliver messages without the distraction of avoidable errors.

PART THREE

The Audit-Report Process

Chapter One:
Issuing Reports Faster

You and your colleagues know that issuing audit reports promptly is essential. But it's taking you weeks—sometimes months—to issue reports once fieldwork is complete. This means that executives aren't getting the real-time information they need. It also means that management either has completed corrective actions before the report is issued or has been able to stall on taking action. Finally, it means that auditors are juggling the tasks for at least three engagements: the report for the completed engagement, the fieldwork for the current engagement, and the planning for the upcoming engagement. How can you deliver accurate, high-quality reports without dragging out the process?

This chapter presents proven strategies for speeding the issuance of audit reports. Included are clear expectations for timeliness, a well-understood and stable report structure, structured preliminary documents, and report-quality checklists. In addition, this chapter touches on reviewing and editing practices aimed at speeding report issuance.

CLEAR EXPECTATIONS

The most powerful thing you can do to ensure prompt reporting is to set expectations and measure progress toward meeting them. We know that we can better improve performance when we measure an activity. Just having a clear expectation for timeliness can improve reporting time.

And what might we expect that measurement to be? World-class internal audit functions—including some large and complex ones—routinely meet the goal of issuing final reports 10 to 14 days after the close of fieldwork. Some, in fact, have trimmed the time to 24 to 48 hours.

Your internal audit function will need to consider a number of factors in setting its expectation for timeliness. These factors include the scope and length of the audit engagement, how many levels of internal-audit management need to review the report, and how many levels of audit-customer management are involved in action planning.

The strategies described in the rest of this chapter can help you meet your timeliness expectations.

WELL-UNDERSTOOD AND STABLE REPORT STRUCTURE

Structure

The report structure should be clear to all: writers, reviewers, and readers. All should be able to look at any section of the report and know immediately what they will find there.

To achieve this clarity, you should avoid generic report-section headings such as *Introduction*. Rather, headings should be fully descriptive of what the section contains. Even a commonly-used heading such as *Background* can be improved by altering it, for example, to *[Audit Entity's] Role and Key Measurements*.

Also, you should opt for more rather than less navigation in the form of headings and sub-headings. Readers today are accustomed to and prefer divided and labeled information. (The success of books covering subjects for *dummies* testifies to this preference.) Using sub-headings to aid navigation is particularly helpful within audit observations and other report sections containing complex or detailed information.

Auditors are fortunate that the professional standards we use provide us with ready-made divisions for audit observations, namely, *criteria, conditions, causes, effects,* and *recommendations* and/or *action plans.* You may opt to use these as the sub-headings or to change the wording to avoid audit jargon. For example, you might replace *criteria* with *requirements* or replace *conditions* with *facts* or *audit results.*

Understanding

To have an impact on cycle time, writers and reviewers need to understand exactly what information goes into each section. You can do several things to engender this understanding:

- Provide training on the structure
- Provide guidance documents that explain the structure
- Offer model reports that execute the structure well

Stability

Once established, the structure should not vary from report to report. Stabilizing the structure in this way benefits writers, reviewers, and audit customers. For writers, a stable structure provides a thought framework, and repeated execution of the structure develops writing speed. For reviewers, a stable structure enables rapid identification of gaps or other deficiencies. And for the readers, a stable structure supports ease of reading. It also allows readers to decide what to read and what to skip—a truth about how readers read that we all should understand.

STRUCTURED PRELIMINARY DOCUMENTS

A preliminary document is a workpaper that auditors use to start writing the audit observation as their understanding of it develops. The best preliminary documents are structured around the components of criteria, conditions, causes, and effects. By structuring them this way, the auditor develops the components that will move forward into the report observation.

However, a preliminary document contains more detail than will likely go forward into the report. Thus, you should structure the preliminary document so it includes a summary for each component, segregated from the detailed information. In this way, you can use the summary in the report and omit the detailed information.

You can further have a positive impact on timeliness by using preliminary documents in the following ways:

- You can share the preliminary document with the audit customer during status meetings to gain concurrence on the accuracy of facts (conditions) and, ideally, on the causes and effects as well.
- You can work out disagreements with the audit customer using the preliminary document to minimize final-report negotiations and changes.
- You can aim to get the wording as close as possible to the anticipated wording of the report observation. This helps to limit wording objections from the audit customer when you provide the report draft.
- You can use the preliminary document to prompt the audit customer's early provision of action plans.

REPORT-QUALITY CHECKLISTS

Report-quality checklists are guides for writers and reviewers. They set quality expectations by listing the desired characteristics of reports. Such checklists should cover everything from the high-level structural issues to tone to the quality and correctness of the writing. Here are the typical inclusions in a quality checklist.

Overall quality

- Accuracy of information
- Appropriateness of formatting

Executive Summary section

- Content of each Executive Summary section (for example, Purpose, Scope, Background, and Opinion or Conclusion)
- Executive Summary's support for the report rating (if a rating is used)

Detailed Report section

- Sequence of the Observations
- Content of the Observations
- Organization of the Observations
- Division or combination of audit issues
- Level of detail
- Content of Recommendations
- Style of Recommendations
- Content of Action Plans or Management Responses

Appendices (if used)

- Content of Appendices
- Format of detailed information

Writing quality

- Paragraphing
- Readability
- Tone
- Grammar
- Punctuation
- Proofreading

You should tailor such a checklist to your own organization. The checklist should align with the structure and focus on the characteristics that add quality to the report. It should prompt writers and reviewers to test report structure along with other significant writing issues.

If appropriate for the organizational culture, you may add scoring to the checklist and use it to rate some number of reports each quarter. Doing so helps track progress toward consistency, quality, and timeliness.

REVIEWING RATHER THAN EDITING

If you are responsible for reviewing and editing, a final timeliness recommendation is to focus on reviewing rather than editing. Editing will get the report that is in front of you issued faster. However, over time, you will continue to spend time editing—report after report—unless you are building the writers' skills. And reviewing—that is providing direction and comments instead of making changes—builds the auditors' writing skills. (See *Part Three, Chapter Two: Reviewing and Editing* for a full discussion of these issues.)

Still, when the deadline is looming, you may need to edit. If you do, make it a practice to go over your edits with the writer.

You've added clarity to your report structure, and you've standardized the structure. Moreover, everyone on staff understands that structure, and you have good ways to explain it and support it with new hires. Preliminary documents are proving to be key. Furthermore, your audit customers appreciate this enhanced communication. Although editing comes easy for you, you're trying to stick to reviewing. Altogether, you're hitting your cycle-time expectation of 21 days, and you're aiming to get that measurement down into world-class time over the next year.

Chapter Two:
Reviewing and Editing

It's late and you're tired, but in front of you is an audit report that has to be issued today. You're dreading the task of reviewing this report because this particular auditor's writing seems to be getting worse with each report she writes. You've extensively marked up all of her reports, and both you and she are getting frustrated. "Why isn't she getting it?" you wonder.

Few documents—and practically no reports—are issued within internal auditing departments without review, and often editing, by someone other than the writer. Perhaps you are the audit manager or director described above, responsible for the quality of those reports and tasked with reviewing each one. Perhaps you're the writer who is required to submit your drafts for review. Or perhaps you're a good writer, so your audit colleagues turn to you for advice.

Whatever your situation, collaborative writing can be a productive, even a developmental, activity for both the writer and the reviewer, or it can be an activity filled with frustrations for both.

This chapter distinguishes reviewing from editing, examines the impacts of each activity on writers and reviewers, describes various writers' and reviewers' mindsets, and provides best practices for effective collaborative writing.

DEFINITIONS, PLEASE

Reviewing is the act of providing feedback on writing without making the changes themselves. A reviewer's comments may be broad or narrow. For example, a reviewer might question the sufficiency of information to support an audit issue, with a comment such as, *What additional data could you summarize to strengthen this point?* A reviewer might make an editorial suggestion, such as, *Try breaking up this long sentence to make it easier to read.* Or a reviewer might make a quite pointed comment, such as, *You need to add a comma here to separate the two parts of this compound sentence.* Regardless of the breadth of the reviewer's comment, the actual change is left in the hands of the writer.

Editing is the act of revising writing. It may include changing the sequence of information, deleting or adding information, revising paragraphs and sentences, and correcting grammar, punctuation, and mechanics. That is, editing changes the document. The edits may be captured electronically (through a feature such as Microsoft® Word's *track changes*) or shown manually (through the traditional red pen). Either way, the editor has taken over the task, leaving the writer to accept or reject the changes. Most writers, of course, accept the changes when they come from their managers.

IMPACTS OF VARIOUS APPROACHES

Both reviewing and editing have advantages and disadvantages for writers and reviewers.

Reviewing

Reviewing has the advantage of placing the primary responsibility for the document in the writer's hands. The writer is closest to the content; thus, the writer is most likely to get the facts right and to draw appropriate conclusions. Reviewing respects the writer's perspective.

Furthermore, reviewing builds the writer's skill. The writer must puzzle out and execute the best solution. Even when the reviewer's comments are quite pointed, the writer is still the one with his or her hands on the keyboard.

A further advantage of reviewing is time saved for the reviewer. This may seem counterintuitive for reviewers who feel that *fixing* the document is the fastest way to deal with its deficiencies. However, reviewing takes less time than does editing. To review, you need only identify the problem; to edit you need not only to identify the problem but also to craft the solution.

A disadvantage is that the reviewing process overall takes more elapsed time. The document has to go back to the writer, and it may have to come back to the reviewer for a second review. Still, reviewing is, in the long term, more efficient if your aim is to build the writer's skills.

Editing

Editing is speedy for the document at hand. That is, editing eliminates returning the document to the writer, so the document can be issued rapidly.

Another perceived advantage of editing is the editor getting precisely what the editor wants, in his or her own style. Such a high degree of stylistic consistency may seem an advantage; however, most readers of internal audit reports are less concerned about stylistic consistency than they are about the accuracy and clarity of the information presented. Furthermore, consistent reports can be produced by having writers adhere to basic specifications for report format, organization, and length. Individual writing-style traits then become less significant.

Most importantly, a steady practice of editing minimizes the opportunity to develop writers' skills. Some editors take time to explain their changes to writers, and this is a good practice. However, these editors are the ones building skills—editing skills—while the writers are bystanders. Few writers improve by simply watching how someone else edits their work.

Finally, poor editing puts the editor in a truly bad light: a skilled writer edited by an unskilled editor will resent the errors. That writer may push back or may, out of frustration, just abdicate responsibility.

WRITERS' AND REVIEWERS' MINDSETS

Nothing impacts the value of collaborative writing more than the mindsets of the writers and the reviewers. When expectations are clear, a collaborative writing process adds quality to the finished document and develops skills in the writer and the reviewer; when expectations are not clear, non-value-added time and frustration result.

Productive mindsets

The most productive mindsets assign primary ownership of the document to the writer. Namely, the writer aims to produce the best document possible before it is passed to the reviewer. The writer does so by ensuring the following:

- The content is accurate and at the appropriate level of detail.
- The document is organized according to expected principles.
- The writing is clear and concise.
- The tone is appropriate.
- The grammar, punctuation, and mechanics are correct.
- The formatting meets expectations or standards.
- The writing is free of typographic errors.

The writer then expects the reviewer to provide insights. These insights often are based the reviewer having more experience as an internal auditor or within the organization. The writer also expects an objective review of the document's organization and writing quality.

The reviewer expects to receive a document that represents the writer's best effort and is free of errors. The reviewer understands that his or her task is to add value from a respectful, objective perspective. This does not mean that the reviewer reads casually or carelessly; rather, the reviewer reads closely and adds comments carefully, aiming to leave the original writing as intact as possible.

Unproductive mindsets

Unfortunately, these productive mindsets can be undermined by misunderstandings about the writer's and the reviewer's roles.

Too often, writers fail to provide reviewers with high-quality documents; rather, such writers produce a draft, which they see as a rough first effort. They fail to take ownership for the quality of the document, expecting and relying on the reviewer to correct the draft. Reviewers fall into the trap, making large and small changes, assuming ownership of the document, and thus reinforcing the writer's draft approach.

Also, reviewers may define themselves as editors. Some reviewers feel that they have never met a document that they could not improve through rewriting. They take over ownership even when the document is objectively satisfactory. This type of compulsive reviewer intimidates inexperienced writers, frustrates good writers, and in the end may cause any writer to stop trying. The writer may think, *Why bother when everything I write gets changed anyway?*

BEST PRACTICES

The following represent best practices for effective collaboration.

The process should be based on reviewing, not on editing. To enable this approach, the writers should agree that the document they deliver will be the best effort they can produce. Furthermore, the writing process should include sufficient time for the reviewers to review and the writers to revise.

The writers and reviewers together should develop a writing-quality checklist that both can use. (See *Part Three, Chapter One: Issuing Reports Faster* for more on report-quality checklists.) The writers and the reviewers should agree that each will use this checklist: the writers to self-check their documents before submitting them for review, and the reviewers as the basis for their reviews.

Reviewers then should agree to edit only in the following circumstances:

- The deadline is so tight that reviewing is impractical. Such editorial changes should be reviewed with the writer after the fact to ensure understanding.
- The change is minor, and the error is one the writer does not usually make.
- The change is a grammatical correction in writing produced by someone writing in a language other than their first language. Such editorial changes also require explanation, but some grammatical and syntactical issues are complex enough that review comments may only frustrate the writer and may fail to result in the necessary change.

You know now that you should have built in more time on the report in front of you, but you resolve to do that the next time around. You also resolve to give up your editing habits and strive to be a reviewer instead. You're sure that adopting better practices will yield a better result and a more satisfactory process for you and the writers whose work you review.

PART FOUR

Other Communications

Chapter One:
Communicating Your Mission

You've worked diligently to shape your internal audit group's mission, including helping your staff shift from a "gotcha!" mentality to a more collaborative approach. It's taken a few years, but you're comfortable that your internal auditors have a clear understanding of how they contribute to the overall governance of the organization and help management achieve objectives while maintaining objectivity. You are supported by your organization's audit committee and especially by the audit committee chair.

But your auditors still encounter skepticism—and sometimes downright hostility—during audit engagements. Also, you feel you are not always "at the table" with senior management when initiatives are under development, so your ability to contribute controls expertise is not being fully tapped.

How do you communicate your mission to your organization? How do you help your organization understand what you do and can do? How do you get across distinctions between auditing and consulting engagements? And how do you build and sustain credibility for your staff and yourself?

This chapter describes how internal auditors may use various types of communications to help others understand internal audit's mission. The chapter first raises the question of why such communications are important. Then, the chapter describes an overall communications plan and suggests some creative approaches to communications: issue updates, presentations-in-a-box, and descriptions of internal audit's services and personnel. Finally, the chapter briefly addresses considerations for maintaining an internal audit web page.

REASONS FOR COMMUNICATING YOUR MISSION

Some internal auditors may decide it's not necessary to be proactive in communicating internal audit's mission. They may feel that their role is clearly defined and understood, or they may feel that marketing themselves is inappropriate. And some internal auditors wish to maintain a distance from the organization because they believe that this distance contributes to objectivity.

However, many internal audit departments find that they accomplish their objectives more effectively and efficiently when the organization fully understands their mission. Encouraging better understanding is particularly desirable when internal audit has shifted or fine-tuned its mission in response to change. Mergers and acquisitions, expanded responsibilities related to overall risk management, changes in staffing, alterations in the audit process itself—all of these may call for you to reach out to the organization by describing or reinforcing your mission.

In addition, misunderstandings about internal audit abound. Those who sporadically interact with internal auditors may have little understanding of your true role and your processes. Such a lack of understanding may contribute to audit-customer defensiveness or resistance. Furthermore, misunderstandings may prevent others—including executives—from seeking you out for your controls expertise.

A COMMUNICATIONS PLAN

A documented communications plan should precede any communications effort. Such a plan starts with an assessment of your communication objectives, your intended audiences, and your key messages. The plan proceeds to decisions about the best media for each communication objective. The plan is then rounded out by the development of a schedule and the assignment of responsibilities.

By starting with the objectives, audiences, and messages, you focus on what you hope to achieve and those with whom you need to communicate. You also narrow that focus by pinpointing the key message for each communication objective.

For this part of the planning, cast a wide net. Explore all the possible objectives you may have for communicating your mission. Areas you might consider include the following:

- Your audit charter: what you are tasked to do by the organization
- Your audit process: how you fulfill your charter, including changes you've made in your process and why
- How you interface with the organization: channels of communication as well as your reporting relationship
- Your audit services: what you provide for the organization, including—if you do so—offering non-audit, consultative advice and in what areas
- Your audit staffing: the expertise and credentials of your audit staff

Once you've established your communication objectives, you can consider media. These are the various channels through which we receive information: written, oral, and visual. Each comprises specific types, and media often are used in combination.

Traditional documents and oral presentations may come to mind first when you consider media. Traditional documents would include reports, memos, and emails; traditional oral presentations would include talks at meetings (often supported by slides) and one-on-one conversations.

While considering media, you should stretch to consider creative ways to use these traditional types as well as ways to incorporate marketing-type and newer media. For example, does your organization hold lunch-and-learn sessions? Should internal audit use social-networking media?

To implement your plan, you'll need to schedule the frequency of the communications. Some communications may be issued on a regular basis, while others may be issued in response to requests or to specific needs. Developing a schedule helps you commit to an ongoing focus on the communications plan.

Finally, you'll need to consider who will own each communication. Consider spreading the ownership among the members of the internal audit staff. Such an approach allows you tap a range of existing skills or to develop new skills among staff members.

ISSUE UPDATES

Your internal audit department is a valuable source of controls expertise for your organization. You likely keep a close eye on risk-and-control trends and emerging issues. Thus, you can be a valued resource for management by highlighting important issues for the organization.

One way to do so is to provide issue updates. These may be sent periodically or sporadically, and they may be delivered via email, included in other organization publications, and/or posted on your organization's internal web page. If you use email messages, issue updates may be sent either to management in general or to particular segments of management, depending on the issue.

In preparing such updates, use a journalistic approach: make your issue updates read like news articles. Consider such journalistic approaches as an attention-grabbing headline, a solid lead paragraph, a top-down writing style, and call-outs.

- An attention-grabbing headline is a compressed statement of the update's main message.
- A solid lead paragraph answers the five W's plus H: who, what, when, where, why, and how.
- A top-down writing style presents a reader-focused summary right after the lead; the remaining paragraphs add detail.
- Call-outs highlight key sentences within the update.

Here is an annotated example of a portion of an issue update that uses a journalistic approach.

> *Example*
>
> State Authority to Require Enhanced Data Security Within a Year (*headline*)
>
> By December of next year (*when*), the State Hospital Oversight Authority (*who*) will require enhanced data security for inpatient and outpatient records (*what*) in all institutions governed by the existing Hospital Data-Security Mandate Act of 20xx (*where*). The enhancements are aimed at keeping pace with hackers' data-intrusion methods (*why*). Hospitals will be expected to meet the new requirements by a combination of automated control—built into hospital systems—and education of hospital personnel (*how*).
>
> | We are positioned well to meet these requirements because of our proactive approach to data security. (*call-out*) |
>
> We at Our Local Hospital are positioned well to meet these new requirements because of our proactive approach to data security, which was developed and implemented through the Full Data Security Project, a joint effort of the Information Technology (IT) Department and Internal Auditing (IA). This project looked ahead to long-term solutions for the security of patient, physician, and staff information. (*reader-focused summary*)

Providing your organization with relevant issue updates can help you communicate your mission. Specifically, you reinforce your role within the governance structure of your organization. You also emphasize that your role can extend beyond conducting audits to being a trusted source for information and assistance.

PRESENTATIONS-IN-A-BOX

Auditors are continually sharing their expertise about internal controls. In fact, they indirectly educate their audit customers each time they conduct an audit. A presentation-in-a-box allows you to deliver such education directly and intentionally.

A presentation-in-a-box is a ready-made presentation that can be delivered at a moment's notice. It usually consists of a slide file, a few handouts, and an outline or script for the presentation. A presentation-in-a-box may be offered during an audit engagement or scheduled for delivery at a separate time.

Topics for which you may want a presentation-in-a-box include the following:

- Overview of governance, risk-management, and controls concepts
- Hallmarks of effective process documentation
- Roles and responsibilities for various compliance activities, such as Sarbanes-Oxley
- Fraud awareness
- Internal audit's mission and role in governance
- Overview of internal audit's own processes

MARKETING-STYLE DESCRIPTIONS OF SERVICES AND PERSONNEL

When asked, you likely can offer an explanation of your services, be they restricted to assurance engagements or expanded to include consulting services. Moreover, your internal audit charter provides detailed descriptions of these activities.

However, you may find it worthwhile to create short, ready-made descriptions that you can provide in various settings. Written in easily-understood language, such descriptions can focus on how your services support the larger organization. Furthermore, they can be produced in an attractive, marketing-style format. You might use such descriptions as handouts at meetings, as part of your opening-meeting information on audit and consulting engagements, and as an add-on to your presentations-in-a-box.

The same can be said for descriptions of personnel. These can be reader-friendly mini-resumes or biographical sketches. They can help everyone from audit customers to management to audit committee members get to know your staff and its capabilities.

Here is an example of a reader-friendly personnel description.

Example

Get to Know an Auditor Mike A. Friend, RN, CIA	
What has been Mike's experience at Our Local Hospital?	Mike has been with us since 20xx. He started his career here as an RN in the Critical Respiratory Care Unit (CRCU), where he received the Team Member of the Month recognition six times. Mike moved on to supervise the nursing staff in CRCU, filling that role for three years. He joined the Internal Audit Department in 20xx.
Why did Mike become an internal auditor?	Mike was intrigued by internal auditing because of the impact it can have on the overall effectiveness of our services. He also found that the analytical skills he developed in nursing were a perfect fit for helping analyze and solve problems from an auditing perspective.
What does the CIA designation mean?	This is the *Certified Internal Auditor* designation. It means that Mike has studied the theory and practice of internal auditing and has passed a rigorous multi-part exam. Mike is a true professional, not only in nursing but also in internal auditing.
In Mike's own words…	*I have taken another step in my career—a step where I can continue to support the health and wellbeing of our patients and the good work of our staff.*

INTERNAL AUDIT WEB PAGE

Many internal audit departments maintain an internal audit web page. However, some have not clearly defined its function. Furthermore, some may not have considered what it takes to use the web page as a tool for communicating with the organization at large.

Your web page may be for your department's use only; if so, its function should be narrowly defined as such. The content, organization, and style of the web page should serve your audit staff alone.

If, on the other hand, you want your web page to serve as a communications tool with the larger organization, carefully consider the following questions:

- What are the goals of the web page?
- Who in the organization is likely to want or need to visit your web page?

- How will you attract and retain the attention of visitors to your web page? What's in it for them?
- On what schedule will various components of the web page be updated?
- Who will keep the web page up to date?

Once these questions are answered, you may consider including many of the communication tools described in this chapter. That is, your web page can be a repository for issue updates, service descriptions, personnel descriptions, and even for the presentations-in-a-box. If you place the latter on your web page, you might consider automating them and adding audio commentary, making the presentations free-standing.

Your mission and organizational role are clear to you and your staff, and now you intend to make them clearer to others in the organization as well. You've got everyone on the staff contributing to some presentations-in-a-box, and you're deciding how you can regularly develop issue updates. You're confident that—when management better understands internal audit—you'll be better able to accomplish your mission.

Chapter Two:
Presenting Clearly

Your chief audit executive has taken a long look at the slide presentations your internal audit staff gives to senior management and executives, and she doesn't like what she sees. These presentations are used at audit opening meetings, audit closing meetings, and at the start of consulting projects. The substance of the presentations is excellent. But your chief audit executive thinks the slides look old-fashioned—even unprofessional—and you agree. She's given you the task of revising them so that their "look" matches the quality of their content. But you're not a graphic designer, so where do you start? What makes slide presentations clear and professional?

This chapter describes best practices for the content and graphic quality of slide presentations.

NOT JUST CUT-AND-PASTE

The best presentation slides are supporting materials. They serve as information anchors not only for your audience but also for those presenting. To build clear and functional slides, think of them in this way: they should not duplicate your hardcopy materials nor should they be a repository for all the information inside your head.

CONTENT

Controlling the amount and style of the content contributes to clear, readable slides.

Amount of content

Six-by-six is a good rule for slide content: put no more than six bullets on a slide, and include no more than six words per bullet. Your slides will be readable, and they will support—not distract from—your presentation.

Style of content

Following the six-by-six rule requires editorial restraint and skill. For example, say you want to convey these three ideas: (1) Our risk-based audit process enables us to focus on the highest-level risks within the organization, (2) The planning of our audit coverage for the year uses a risk-based process, and (3) During each engagement, we apply the risk-based process as well. You have fewer than six bullets, but each one is longer than six words. Here's how you might compress these three statements into readable bullets on a slide titled *Risk-Based Audit Process*: (1) Focuses on highest-level risks, (2) Annual audit planning approach, (3) During audits, application of risk-based process.

You're partway there, but you now need to edit so that the bulleted items are parallel: each must use the same grammatical form. Parallelism enhances clarity, making it easier for your audience to scan the list and to absorb the ideas. You might revise your example slide *Risk-Based Audit Process* like this: (1) Focused on highest-level risks, (2) Used in annual audit planning, and (3) Applied during each audit engagement.

What if you have more than six bullet items on a topic? You have two choices: combine some of the items to stay within the six-by-six rule, or make more than one slide. Combining will challenge you to edit well. On the other hand, making more than one slide will challenge you to break the content rationally. Further, making more than one slide may mean you have to backtrack during the presentation. Despite these challenges, repeatedly violating the six-by-six rule leads to audience overload.

GRAPHIC QUALITY

Slide programs provide tempting options for fonts, graphics, and animation. But just because you can do something graphically doesn't mean that you should. Poor decisions about graphic quality distract from rather than enhance a presentation.

Four graphic-quality considerations will support the content quality of your slides:

- Readable colors
- Readable fonts
- Appropriate graphics
- Appropriate animation

Readable colors

An infinite variety of background and font colors is available, so how do you choose?

First, consider the environment in which the slides will be projected. If they will be used in a medium to large space (for example, during a conference presentation or a seminar), light letters on a dark background are easier to read because a bright, white background with dark letters is visually fatiguing on a large screen. In a smaller setting, however, dark letters on a light background work well.

Second, avoid color combinations that make for hard reading. The presenter who chose an emerald green background with bright yellow letters left his audience with a headache rather than with memorable content.

Third, as you develop your color palette, limit the number of colors to three or four, and use them consistently. That is, ensure that headings are always the same color and that bulleted text and sub-bulleted text follows a consistent color pattern. Often, using only one color for all of the text—regardless of its position as heading, bullet, or sub-bullet—is the least distracting choice.

Finally, keep in mind that you can alter the colors in any standard template your slide program offers, and you can re-color clip-art graphics as well. Doing so makes such clip art an integral and pleasing component of your presentation.

Readable fonts

As with colors, fonts are available in almost infinite variety. For clarity's sake, don't be tempted: use one font throughout the presentation, altering font size or font characteristics (bolding or italics) to make distinctions where needed.

A key distinction is between *serif* and *sans serif* fonts. *Serif* fonts are characterized by variations in the thickness of the lines that make up the letters and by small ornaments (these are the *serifs*) on letters; Times New Roman is a typical *serif* font. *Sans serif* fonts are characterized by lack of variation (or only slight variation) in the thickness of lines and by lack of ornamentation (thus, *sans serif*, meaning *without serifs* in French); Arial is a typical *sans serif* font.

Although printed text is more readable in *serif* fonts, projected text is more readable in *sans serif* fonts. This is because *serif* fonts often break up when projected: the ornaments become slightly fuzzy distractions.

Finally, you should select a font that does not contain what are called ligatures. Specifically, some fonts place certain letters so close together that parts of the letters touch; for example, side-by-side t's may appear to be crossed by a single line. Avoid these fonts. They are difficult to read when projected.

Appropriate graphics

It's true that a picture can be worth a thousand words. Graphics include the pictures we call charts and graphs as well as images such as logos, clip art, photographs, and video. Charts and graphs compress detailed information and highlight messages and trends within the information; images convey impressionistic messages.

In deciding which chart or graph to use, consider the message you aim to deliver. Each type of chart or graph has a best use. For example, line graphs highlight changes or trends in one or several elements over time, bar graphs highlight comparisons, pie charts show proportional distribution of data, and flowcharts represent chronological order and decision points.

A projected chart or graph must be simple enough to make the point at a glance. For example, a line graph will confuse rather than clarify when it has more than 10 hash marks on either axis, has more than three lines on the chart, or needs explanatory footnotes.

Finally, check the chart or graph for visual clarity. For example, if you are relying on dashed lines or patterned bars, ensure that they can be distinguished one from the other.

Images are powerful, and you should consider any images from all perspectives, using these questions as a starting point:

- Does the image contribute to the message of the slide? A presentation where every slide has an image—regardless of its appropriateness—not only is challenging to create but also is distracting to audiences as they ponder what the random images mean. When in doubt, omit the image.
- Does the image appropriately represent the diversity of your organization?
- Does the image invoke the appropriate emotion? Images are inherently evocative; ensure that the emotion of the image matches the message of the slide.

Finally, when using clip art, choose images from the same family. For example, avoid mixing cartoons or iconic images with more literal images. Staying within image families will be less challenging if you use images sparingly and appropriately.

Appropriate animation

You can make slides, text, graphics, and images enter, disappear, flash, and otherwise dance all over the screen. Don't do it. Use animation as you use graphics: to support the messages. Your aim is not to entertain your audience or to keep them guessing about what clever thing will happen on the next slide. (In fact, audiences today are so sophisticated that almost nothing you do with animation will impress them.) Rather, you will diminish the effectiveness of your message. They may even wonder how you had the time to build in all that animation.

Use the simplest animation possible. For example, use bullet-by-bullet builds when you want to synchronize the delivery of the bullets to a fuller explanation of each. In contrast, you likely do not need a bullet-by-bullet build if you are advancing all the bullets with little to say about each (or if you are having the slide program automatically do so).

Animate your graphics when the animation adds something to the message. If, for example, you want to show a dramatic comparison, an animated bar chart can help drive home the comparison.

Finally, if your audience has the printed presentation in front of them, remember that what you are revealing has already been revealed to them. Use the animation sparingly to avoid unnecessarily slowing down your delivery.

ALIGNMENT WITH YOUR AUDIENCE AND YOUR ORGANIZATION

As with any communication, your reality check for slides should be to view them through your audience's eyes. Are they readable? Are they clear? Do they support your message? Do they contain any distractions? Will the audience understand?

Finally, to use your slides for maximum effect, ensure that they take on the style and look of your organization. Using your organization's logo and color scheme telegraphs that you are an integral part of the organization. Matching the formality or informality of your organization sends a similar message. Does your organization like charts and graphs? Use them. Does it rely on visual imagery? Include images.

By aligning with the audience and the organization—and by following the best practices for content and graphics—you've been able to produce polished, up-to-date presentations that made the chief audit executive proud.

CPSIA information can be obtained at www.ICGtesting.com
Printed in the USA
LVOW03s1950050215

425896LV00002B/4/P